Company East India

# Proceedings at a General Court of Proprietors of East-India Stock,

held at the India-house, on Friday, November 7, 1783, relative to the Hon. Warren Hastings, governor general of Bengal

Company East India

**Proceedings at a General Court of Proprietors of East-India Stock,**
*held at the India-house, on Friday, November 7, 1783, relative to the Hon. Warren Hastings, governor general of Bengal*

ISBN/EAN: 9783337012564

Printed in Europe, USA, Canada, Australia, Japan

Cover: Foto ©Suzi / pixelio.de

# PROCEEDINGS

AT A

# GENERAL COURT, &c.

# PROCEEDINGS

AT A

# GENERAL COURT

OF

PROPRIETORS

OF

# EAST-INDIA STOCK,

HELD AT THE

INDIA-HOUSE,

ON

FRIDAY, NOVEMBER 7, 1783,

RELATIVE TO THE

## Hon. WARREN HASTINGS,

GOVERNOR GENERAL OF BENGAL.

LONDON:
Printed for J. DEBRETT, opposite BURLINGTON-HOUSE, PICCADILLY.
M.DCC.LXXXIII.

# INTRODUCTION.

IN order to elucidate the following important debate, we wiſh to bring to the recollection of the public, the following circumſtances:

On the 28th of May, 1782, the late Lord Advocate of Scotland propoſed a reſolution in the Houſe of Commons, "That it was the duty of the Court of Directors to recal Mr. Haſtings from the Government of Bengal."

On the 18th of June following, the Court of Proprietors reſolved, that the Directors were not to carry into effect any reſolution they might come to for the removal of Mr. Haſtings, without laying it before a General Court.

On the 23d of October, 1782, after violent debates at the India Houſe, thirteen Directors voted for the removal of Mr. Haſtings — ten Directors oppoſed the meaſure, and ſeven of theſe gentlemen proteſted againſt it in the ſtrongeſt manner.

On the 24th, this reſolution was laid before a General Court, when it was fully and ably debated, and the following motion was made by Governor Johnſtone, and ſeconded by Samuel Smith, jun. Eſq. member for Ilcheſter.

That it appears to this court, from inconteſtable evidence drawn from the records of the Com-

Company, and ſupported by the unanimous opinion of the Houſe of Commons, that the war in which we are now engaged with the Marattas, "was evidently founded on the ſentiments of the Court of Directors, conveying demands on the Maratta adminiſtration greatly exceeding the conditions of the treaty of Poorunder; which ſentiments of the Court of Directors opened the firſt deſign of ſending a detachment from Bengal to the Malabar coaſt;" and that conſequently it would be the height of injuſtice to lay the blame of that war, or the evils which have flowed from it, upon Mr. Haſtings, when it appears, "that the diſſatisfaction of the Court of Directors expreſſed at the treaty of Poorunder, in their letters to Bengal of the 5th of February, and to Bombay of the 16th of April, 1777, gave the ſtrongeſt encouragement to both preſidencies, to ſeize the ſlighteſt pretence of provocation from the miniſters of the Maratta ſtates, to renew their engagements with Ragobah." Neither have the meaſures adopted by Mr. Haſtings, in conſequence of ſuch inſtructions, ever received the ſlighteſt cenſure from the ſaid Court of Directors; in conſideration whereof, it is now recommended to the Court of Directors to reſcind their late reſolution reſpecting the removal of Warren Haſtings, Eſq. Governor General of Bengal;

Bengal; more eſpecially as it appears to this Court that, according to the laſt official diſpatches from Bengal, dated the 8th April, 1782, the proſpect of peace with the Marattas was then propitious, becauſe it ſeemed to be wiſhed for by all the Maratta ſtates; becauſe hoſtilities with them had ceaſed for many months, and that a peace had actually been concluded with Mahdajee Sindia, one of the principal chiefs of that confederacy; and farther, that the Government General of Bengal were uſing every means in their power to effect a general pacification; and that the conduct of the ſaid Government General, tending to produce a general pacification, or to unite and ſupport, by powerful reſources, a general confederacy of the country powers, to defeat the combination of Hyder Ally and the French, (ſuppoſing the ſaid Hyder Ally ſhall not accept of the reaſonable terms of accommodation which have been offered to him in conſequence of his propoſals for peace) merits the warmeſt approbation of this Court; and that therefore it would be evidently injurious to the intereſts of the Company and the nation to remove any of thoſe principal ſervants of the Company, now diſcharging their duty with ſuch uncommon exertions, ability, and unanimity, or to ſhake the authority repoſed in them by the legiſlature and the Company,

pany, at a period ſo critical, when the proſperity of the Britiſh intereſts in India will depend, in a great meaſure, on the confidence which the native princes of the country may place in the Government General of Bengal."

Several Gentlemen who were preſent expreſſed a wiſh that this motion ſhould be determined by a ballot, and the friends of Mr. Haſtings being very deſirous to take the ſenſe of the Eaſt-India Company upon ſo important a queſtion, in the fulleſt and the faireſt manner, very readily acquieſced, and ſome of them ſigned the requiſition for the ballot. On the 31ſt of October the ballot was taken, and the numbers ſtood as follow:

| | |
|---|---|
| For the queſtion — — | 428 |
| Againſt it — — | 75 |
| Majority in favour of Mr. Haſtings | 353 |

This was the laſt proceeding in 1782, relative to Mr. Haſtings. Nothing was done in Parliament; and in conſequence of the intelligence received from Bengal by the Suprize Packet, Governor Johnſtone and eight Proprietors addreſſed a letter to the Court of Directors on the 29th of October, deſiring that a General Court might be called to conſider the late advices from Bengal. It was fixed by the Directors to meet on Friday the 7th inſtant.

# PROCEEDINGS

AT A

# GENERAL COURT, &c.

*At a numerous and respectable Meeting of the Proprietors of East-India Stock, held at their House in Leadenhall-Street, on Friday, November 7, 1783; among many other distinguished Characters present were, his Grace the Archbishop of York, General Oglethorpe, the Honourable Mr. Greville, &c. &c. &c.*

AFTER some private business of little importance, Sir *Henry Fletcher* informed the Court of Proprietors of the reason of their being summoned — It was to consider the late advices from Bengal, in consequence of a letter from nine proprietors — but before they should enter on the subject for which they were assembled, he begged leave to propose that the petition to the House of Commons, presented

 last

laſt ſeſſion, in conſequence of which they had received certain aid, but not all they required, might be renewed. He ſtated the circumſtance to which the petition particularly alluded. They had prayed for liberty to borrow 1,500,000l. Of this ſum they had been ſuffered to borrow 500,000l. and temporary aid was given them for the 1,000,000l. but that aid they wiſhed to be permanent — and the ſpecific amount of the relief prayed for would make the only difference between the preſent and the laſt petition.

This buſineſs being finiſhed, and the letter read, Governor *Johnſtone* addreſſed the Chairman —

Sir HENRY FLETCHER,

The letter which has been read for calling the General Court, has already informed the proprietors of the purpoſe for which they are aſſembled. Thoſe advices from the Eaſt Indies which they are to take under conſideration, have been publiſhed in the newſpapers, and extracts of all the material intelligence they convey have lain open for the peruſal of the proprietors, as appears by the public advertiſement for calling the Court; otherwiſe in point of form, I ſhould begin by reading the advices to which I mean to refer, before I propoſe the motion I intend to ſubmit to the conſideration of the Court: but as the reading of voluminous public diſpatches is often diſguſting to ſuch aſſemblies, when the matter under diſcuſſion is of public notoriety, and where all who are anxious to underſtand the particulars have had an opportunity

nity ſo to do, I ſhall therefore adopt another mode of proceeding, which is, by giving the reaſons for the motion I ſhall propoſe before I ſit down; and then referring to the particular articles in the diſpatches on which the motion is grounded, that they may be read by the clerk.

The taſk I have impoſed upon myſelf is, indeed, attended with much difficulty, not from want of ſufficient and ſuperabundant matter to vindicate the motion, with which I mean to conclude, giving thanks to Mr. Haſtings and his council, for the exertions they have made in the public cauſe; but from that diſpoſition of party and faction in the ſtruggles for power, which has diſtracted this community in every part: to which I impute our late misfortunes, much more than to the exertions of our enemies. This ſpirit has gone forth to ſuch a rancorous degree that it is hardly poſſible, in the opinion of ſome, to give praiſe to one man, without throwing cenſure on others: but this cenſure is far from being my intention; it is rather my wiſh to heal the diſſentions that have prevailed, and to correct that ſpirit ſo detrimental to the community, than by any irritation to inflame it. I am not dexterous in my choice of words; but, once for all, I declare this to be my meaning. Nevertheleſs, if there are men of ſuch malignity of diſpoſition, that they cannot view the great actions of men with whom they have been connected in political enmity, without conſidering it as a reproach to themſelves, I freely acknowledge I would rather incur the enmity of ſuch men, than withold, as far as I am able to enforce it, that tribute of applauſe which is due to thoſe who have greatly ſerved their country. It has been my lot, Sir, in the ſtruggles which this country has undergone againſt her numerous enemies, to attach myſelf chiefly to thoſe characters who were willing boldly to meet the danger, not tamely to ſubmit to the indignities of our enemies; nor, by croaking deſpondency in the hour of diſtreſs, when nothing but animated exertion could ſave us, unman themſelves, and diſpirit their countrymen. It has been the fortune, or misfortune of other men in this community, to employ themſelves in curious inveſtigation to diminiſh the luſtre of thoſe characters; but, thank God! juſt as the effects of their laborious reſearches were likely to burſt on my friends, by the news of ſome great and glorious action, achieved by thoſe perſons, arriving, their reputation has been ſaved, and the men who would have blaſted their fame have been obliged to join in the public applauſe. Such was the caſe of Lord Rodney, who, when abſent in the ſervice of his country, had a committee of the Houſe of Commons ſitting in ſevere ſcrutiny on his actions at St. Euſtatius. The report was made by the ſame right honourable gentleman who has favoured the world with the Ninth Report, and other papers, criminating Mr. Haſtings — nay, the day of his condemnation was fixed, and his recal had already taken place, when the accounts of the glorious 12th of April came to raiſe the ſpirit of his friends,

friends, and to abash the malignity of his enemies. In like manner, after the inquisitorial proceedings of the Select Committee had been given to the House of Commons, and industriously circulated to the public, to prejudice the character of Mr. Hastings—after he had been represented in a great national assembly as a public robber, and most notorious oppressor — after his enemies had, held out the hopes he had given of saving our possessions in the East Indies as so many scenes in a series of delusions, there comes, in a moment, as critical in his favour as the victory of the 12th of April was in that of Lord Rodney — an account of the Maratta treaty, settling and commanding the peace of India, the retreat of Tippoo Saib from the Carnatic, the taking of the province of Bednore, and the surrender of Mangalore; which leaves no longer any doubt of the triumph of our arms, and the stability of our possessions in the East. The conduct of Mr. Hastings and Lord Rodney, may be compared to that of Sylla, when prosecuting the war against Mithridates. Being informed by one of the officers of the proceedings of Marius, he was asked how he could remain in Asia while such persecutions were carrying on against him at Rome? Sylla made answer, "It is by this I am making the most cruel war against Marius. I will first conquer the enemies of the Republic, and then return to Rome and punish Marius." Upon such an occasion as the present, I would recommend to those who have been the professed enemies of Mr. Hastings, to follow the exact line they did in the case of my Lord Rodney. They were the first to run to the senate, and the first to propose public thanks upon so great an event: and the orator, upon whose representations they had chiefly relied for their former opinion, declared that he could no longer look through such a blaze of glory at the faults he had discovered, and was ready to cover them with the ensigns which he had taken from the enemy. In like manner, admitting for the sake of obtaining unanimity in the motion I shall make, that Mr. Hastings has had some faults in his conduct, yet I desire that those who were formerly disposed to view him in that light will now cover those errors with the Maratta treaty, with the standards of Tippoo Saib, with the ensigns of Bednore and Mangalore. In the same spirit I would advise those who are so charmed with the wit of the Ninth Report of the Select Committee, to read, as an antidote, the history of the transactions I have enumerated. During the last recess of parliament, I have often heard it asked, have you read the Ninth Report? If ever that question is put again, I advise the friends of Mr. Hastings to make no other answer than this: have you read the Maratta Treaty? In great national affairs, like this under our consideration, upon which the fate of an empire depends, it is in vain to call upon me to look at little specks in the conduct of such men; they may be true or false; I will disdain to consider them at such a moment, when my heart should be filled with the effusions of joy and gratitude.

tude. It was left for the *Examiner* and his aſſociates, to find out that the Duke of Marlborough had given a contract to this or that man improperly, but who, on receiving the account of the battle of Blen heim or Ramillies, would have ſtopped the tribute of his praiſe and admiration, upon ſo trifling a tale. The Court of Directors ſhould be particularly cautious, not to admit any prejudice in their minds from the reports of the Select Committee. It is well known, that as ſtrong reports as could be framed, were brought down by that reſpectable Committee againſt two of your own body; * but when the accuſation came to be ſifted, it appeared ſo frivolous and ill founded, that the framers of the report were aſhamed to bring the iſſue to a public diſcuſſion and deciſion. If this has happened reſpecting men on the ſpot, how much more may we ſuſpect the labours of that diſintereſted body, reſpecting a man at the diſtance of four thouſand leagues? But, I ſhould be ſorry to be underſtood, as meaning to inſinuate that actions, however great in themſelves ſhould cover any injuſtice to individuals. Theſe are ſubjects of proper diſcuſſion for the courts of juſtice; or if Mr. Haſtings, in the preſſing exigency of his ſituation, has exacted more men or money from any perſon, than equity or ſound policy will warrant in the defence of the State; let the Court of Directors order compenſation when the peace is eſtabliſhed. All I contend for at preſent is, that the ſituation was critical, the aſſiſtance requiſite; and if there appears ſome fault in the mode of enforcing the payments, it was an exceſs of zeal in

* Mr. Sulivan and Sir William James.

your

your ſervice, and not for his own emolument; therefore it ſhould not ſtop the current of your approbation on this day.

But, Sir, the General Court of Proprietors are more particularly called upon to expreſs their ſentiments, upon the late advices from the Eaſt Indies; they have been vilified, traduced, and abuſed; nay, all their privileges, ſecured by ſacred charters, threatened to be taken away by that aſſembly, which ought to be the guardians and protectors of public rights, becauſe they had offered to interfere againſt a torrent of intemperate proceedings, and ſupport this very man in his ſituation, who has now fulfilled their expectations, and ſo completely vindicated their character and his own. Though I can by no means recommend the ſpirit of exultation, where I wiſh to heal the wounds of diſcord, yet I cannot, on the other hand, aſſume that modeſty, which would deny bringing thoſe tranſactions to the recollection of the public. If this court had not interpoſed, firſt by the reſolution in June, and afterwards by that in October, 1782, I believe there is none acquainted with the affairs of the Eaſt, who will not allow, that inſtead of rejoicing for public events, we ſhould have had cauſe to mourn over misfortunes, worſe than the loſs of America: even you, Sir, who was then of opinion, that the Maratta treaty was a deluſion, and that the aſpect of our affairs, as we had painted them, in the motion for reſcinding that reſolution of the Court of Directors, which had diſ-

miſſed

missed Mr. Hastings, will now acknowledge it has been attended with the best effects. Since, then, all our prognostics have proved true, since the course of events has exceeded the expectations of the most sanguine, it would be unworthy our characters not to claim the merit of our conduct under such circumstances.

That the subsequent part of my discourse may be better understood, I shall here read the motion with which I intend to conclude, and when the three resolutions are taken together, I shall not consider them as that part of my conduct in life, which gives me the least satisfaction, in having had the honour to propose them.*

As far as I have been able to catch the pulse of the public, I understand there will be little opposition to any part of the motion I have read, except the conclusion. Government are very apt, when they chuse, to interfere in an extraordinary manner in the affairs of the East-India Company, to hold a language in which I do not entirely disagree with them; that the affairs of the East are now of such magnitude and consequence to the state, that every man in high station in that country may be considered as the immediate servant of the public; but I observe this language is more frequently assumed when they are pleased to throw censure, than to communicate praise. The thanks of the House of Commons have been given

* Here the motion inserted at the end of the speech was read.

to Sir Eyre Coote, in my opinion moſt deſervedly. The thanks of that Houſe have likewiſe been given to Sir Edward Hughes, with equal juſtice; but great and illuſtrious as theſe characters are, noble as their exertions muſt ever appear, will any one, who underſtands the tranſactions of the Eaſt Indies, ſay they have performed greater public ſervices than Mr. Haſtings? Sir Eyre Coote will not ſay ſo; for, on the contrary, he has told you, the ſaving of the Carnatic has been owing to the extraordinary exertions of the Governor General. Sir Edward Hughes will not ſay ſo, who, with a peculiar modeſty, forgetting his own merit, has dwelt with pleaſure and admiration on that of his friend, Governor Haſtings. If thoſe officers, acting on the ſpot, afford us this teſtimony of approbation, and the concluſion of the ſcene vindicates their opinion, ſhall we believe them, or the judgment of a Committee who have not been farther than the avenues of St. James's? Neither do I ſee how it is poſſible with juſt reaſoning to aſſent to the firſt part, and deny the concluſion. It may be ſaid, however, what motives have this Committee to miſlead the public? It does not become me to enter into the motives of men; the ſtruggles for power are often productive of the worſt miſchiefs to the public, and the moſt cruel injuſtice to indviduals. It is poſſible alſo that thoſe gentlemen feel none of the reſentments they would endeavour to raiſe in our minds. Men, moving in the higher orbits, ſeldom enter the circle of inveteracy; that is left to the inferior orders of men, if they are weak enough to be drawn into the eddy; but what we have lately

ſeen

seen may teach us to avoid this situation. Perhaps if Mr. Hastings had quitted his office of Governor-General of Bengal, we should have heard no more complaints against him; he might have remained as quiet as any other displaced minister, nay, I should not be surprized if his greatest enemy, succeeding to his office, should, in a short time, pronounce his eulogium, and that all our squabbles at this end of the town should end in as pleasing a coalition, as that which has appeared at St. Stephen's. If I am pressed still farther to explain the motives of the Committee, I should say, that I consider the whole as the labours of the principal member of that Committee, and that I apprehend the enmity he has taken up against Mr. Hastings, arises, as I have said in another place, from the tenderness of his mind, and his extreme humanity, which does not permit him to view, with his usual judgement, those scenes of horror which are incident to war. There is hardly a campaign under the mildest officer that does not exhibit scenes, which when painted by a lively imagination, are not sufficient to make us sick of existence; but when those scenes are examined, with the causes that produced them, and the effects that followed, and the necessity which impressed, as the best means to attain the end, the hatred against the person who directed the execution is removed. When the King of Prussia burnt the beautiful suburbs of Dresden, when Sylla ordered his troops to set fire to Rome to drive Marius from the Capitol; in considering only the horrors and devastation which ensued, our minds are apt to revolt againſt the man who could iſſue ſuch orders; and, accordingly, there are many philoſophic writings which have condemned thoſe acts, while other writers on the art of war have praiſed the magnanimity and promptitude of ſpirit which directed them. In the ſame way I apprehend the ſtory of Cheyt Sing has been miſunderſtood, by not conſidering the whole of the tranſaction, as neceſſary to the ſtate of the war, and the preſervation of our poſſeſſions in the Eaſt; and when we come to reflect that this is the only quarter of the globe in which the Britiſh arms have ſuſtained their luſtre without loſing territory, we ſhould be more cautious in imputing blame to the Governor General, who has preſerved them; or in withholding our praiſe for his having ſo done;—if I look to North America, the proſpect is too melancholy; if I caſt my eye to the Weſt Indies, a number of iſlands appear under the flags of our enemies;—if I go to the Mediterranean, I ſee Minorca loſt: it is in the Eaſt alone we have ſuſtained the ſhock with credit; it will hardly be ſaid we have reſiſted the power of our enemies by the wiſdom of our councils at home: ſuppoſing they had ſhewn ſufficient ſagacity in that reſpect near their immediate controul, the diſtance of our poſſeſſions in the Eaſt Indies renders the direction of the reſources of that country impoſſible. It is therefore owing to the government exiſting on the ſpot. Under ſuch circumſtances, if it were only to prevent the invidious parallel, I ſhould hope his Majeſty's Miniſters would not with-hold their tribute of thanks upon ſuch an occaſion.—Whoever will trace the progreſs of the negociation with the Marattas

rattas

rattas from the beginning to the conclusion, the means applied to bring about that event, will find sufficient cause to excite his admiration, and to extinguish any malevolence he may entertain against Mr. Hastings.—There is a degree of spirit and perspicuity through the whole of that business, that makes me, while I rejoice it was under the management of such able hands, wish for a moment the same judicious, active councils could have been communicated to other parts that stood in equal need of them. To trouble the Court with a long citation is always disagreeable to popular assemblies; nevertheless, there is one letter, although of some length, which I cannot refrain from reading, as conveying an idea of that determined spirit which pervaded the whole. The Court will be pleased to observe, that this letter was written to Mr. Anderson, at a period when all others, except Mr. Hastings, were ready to sink into despondency.

(C O P Y.)

*Fort William, Dec.* 4, 1782.

My Dear Anderson,

I Have received yours of the 13th ult.—It is near a month since your letters informed me, that the delivery of the ratified treaty had been promised in fifteen days, and repeated and positive assurances given by Mahdajee Sindia, that his engagements should be fulfilled to your entire satisfaction, or something to that effect, for I have not your letters

by

by me.—If, when you have received this letter, the ratification has not been made, nor Sindia afforded the proofs, whatever they may be, of his fidelity to his engagements, and ability to maintain them himself, and enforce them on others, I shall pay no attention to his future declarations. Had I the power to act from myself alone, I should bring this business to a very short issue. Let us, however, do what we can.—Tell Sindia, but tell him in person, and in my name; 1st, That you have continued too long with him for the honour of our government, if you were only to be the attendant on his person; 2d, That it is necessary to come to a full explanation, and a determinate one, on the points which remain to be adjusted, and for which alone you have been permitted to remain so long with him; 3d, That these points are, first, the ratification of the treaty; and, secondly, a plan of co-operation against Hyder Ally; 4th, That we have expected the former only as it led to the latter, not considering it necessary to the confirmation of the Peace, which by our ratification of the general treaty, and its conclusion by him under the full powers which he possessed is as fixed and binding as the most solemn of all possible sanctions could make it; 5th, That until the treaty is ratified, we shall consider him in his own person as the party to it, and when it is ratified, as the guarantee; but the state bound equally in either case, the form of the ratification being his concern, not ours; 6th, That we are satisfied with our alliance with him; and prefer his name and faith to any

other

other for the ſecurity of the engagements of his nation; 7th, That the general treaty was concluded and executed ſeven months ago, and ratified by us on the inſtant of its receipt; 8th, That the procraſtinating ſpirit of the Marattas, which is proverbial, in all their negociations and concerns with others, has already been the cauſe of one renewal of hoſtilities with the Engliſh, in ſpite of the laboured endeavours of this government to prevent it, and has always a tendency to produce the like conſequences by the diſtruſt inſeparable from ſuch appearances; 9th, That I acquit him of this national cenſure, having found him decided and conſiſtent in every tranſaction which has paſſed between us; and which depended on himſelf alone; 10th, That therefore this remonſtrance is intended for others, with whom we have no connection but through him; 11th, That General Sir Eyre Coote having come to Bengal for the recovery of his health, expects to be able to return to the Carnatic in the beginning of the next month; 12th, That we ſhall in the mean time concert with him the plan of his operations there, whether for peace or war, and give him final inſtructions; 13th, That Hyder himſelf is deſirous of peace, and would agree to it on eaſy conditions; 14th, That his reſources are greatly exhauſted, his army reduced in numbers, and diſcontented; 15th, That the Carnatic, which afforded them a ſubſiſtence, and the incitements of plunder, is now a deſert, and more unprofitable to them than to us; 16th, That we have received large reinforcements of ſoldiers, of the

King's

King's own army from England, which lie inactive, because we are waiting the determination of the Maratta government, not chusing to involve ourselves in any designs which might eventually impede or embarrass our engagements with them; 17th, That it is therefore my desire to know, and I conjure him to tell me with that sincerity which has hitherto marked and done honour to his character, whether the engagements which we are willing to conclude with the Peshwa against our common enemy, can be formed and executed in this season, or whether it is impracticable; 18th, That in this act we must require the sanction of the Peshwa's name, and the concurrence of the minister to give it its due influence and credit; and for the same reason, I wish for the ratification of the treaty likewise, because the world will not believe them to be in earnest while they with-hold it; 19th, That I wish to bring our contest with Hyder to an issue, while we have a superiority in strength, as there is a probability that he will be joined by a powerful armament from France in the next year, which may enable him to bid defiance to our united efforts, if delayed so long; —20, That if they will engage in a plan of immediate co-operation with us, we will make that our object: —21, But if they will not, we will take care of ourselves; —22, That we make no scruple of avowing our wants, because we know theirs to be at least equal to them; since the total loss of the Carnatic, were we to lose it, would be no real loss to us; it would indeed be a loss of credit, and injure our national character by involving the ruin of an old and faithful ally; but our substantial possessions would acquire an additional value from it, Hyder is in possession of a large portion of Marratta dominions, and with the conquest of the Carnatic (an event which I only suppose for argument) would be in a condition to make an easy prey of the rest of the Decan; but if he is only freed from the war with the English, and left at liberty to carry all his forces towards the Kristna, he will not only be able to secure his new possessions in that quarter, but add to them.

I rely on your firmness and address to give this remonstrance complete effect. It is certainly *my* wish to prosecute the war against Hyder to his destruction; but if the Marattas will not assist us, our Forces and resources in the Carnatic are not equal to a war with him and his allies the French; and it will be more for our interest, and even credit, to make peace with him. — This alternative I have therefore resolved to adopt *for myself*. — The General, I believe, inclines to a peace, and would be pleased to be the instrument of effecting it. — These are my own sentiments; make what use of them you please. — Those of my colleagues in this matter I have not consulted.

I am,

My dear Anderson,

Your most affectionate Friend,

(Signed) WARREN HASTINGS.

This letter had its effect, and was the principal cause of bringing matters to a speedy conclusion.— As to the latter part of the motion, it is necessary to declare as my own sentiments, and the sentiments of those with whom I am acting, that we do not mean, as has been industriously given out in the world, to continue Mr. Hastings in the perpetual government of Bengal; on the contrary, it is our wish that his successor shall be appointed; but until a proper successor should be found, we do not wish our affairs should be left in confusion before the arrangements necessary upon a peace establishment shall have taken place; we think also for obvious reasons, that Mr. Hastings is the fittest person to carry these regulations into execution: whoever his successor may be, it can be no dimunition of his dignity, nor any loss in fullfilling the purposes of his commission, to hear and see the plans Mr. Hastings may have adopted; so far from wishing a successor may not be appointed, we are desirous it may take place. Mr. Hastings has formally announced his wish to re-visit his native country, and desired a successor might be appointed; but we are jealous in considering who that person may be. The maintaining dominion at such a distance, is one of the most wonderful scenes in human society, it can only be held by the exercise of the utmost wisdom: this reflection, Sir, must often occur to your mind in moving the goose-quill with which you give or take away a kingdom at the other side of the globe. It is not every person who may make a figure at a court, that is fit for such a trust.

The numerous qualities which are requiſite, are hardly to be found united in the ſame perſon. Our poſſeſſions in the Eaſt Indies ſeem now to be our beſt ſtake, the chance of holding them muſt not be tampered with — In this choice neither favour or affection, but real efficient qualities ſhould prevail. His Majeſty may give titles and honours, but he cannot communicate the wiſdom and experience which are requiſite to a Governor General of Bengal, where the want of local knowlege, if the choice ſhould fall on one who has never been in the country, can only be made up from that general knowledge and experience, which is capable of applying its reflections to every ſituation in life. — Such men are not to be met with in every club of this great city, even if we proceed in our ſearch to thoſe in St. James's Street; perhaps they muſt be ſought for in the ſhade of retreat. That the proprietors of Eaſt-India ſtock ſhould have ſome opinion in the choice, is what I maintain; that they ſhould alone direct, is more than I contend for. — To fall ſo low as we are placed by the compiler of the Ninth Report, is a ſituation to which I never will ſubmit, until the plan he propoſes of annihilating our privileges, ſhall be carried into execution. It is curious to examine the conceit and the principles which are apparent in that performance. He tells you that all the Reformations which Parliament have attempted hitherto, have been deſtructive of the end propoſed; and yet, without drawing the natural concluſion, of precaution in breaking ancient inſtitutions with too much temerity;

 where

where the united wiſdom of the nation has failed, this gentleman is for levelling every barrier in the conſtitution of our body, and breaking in pell-mell upon thoſe rights and privileges which have ſuſtained the intercourſe of the Eaſt ſo long, which conquered the dominion in queſtion, and has preſerved it under the late deſperate attacks.

Another reaſon for conceiving the motion in thoſe words, is to avoid any ſhock between the juriſdiction of the Court of Directors, and the Governor General of Bengal; where the dignity of both ſeem to be committed — it is not my wiſh to enter into the controverſy. If Mr. Haſtings is requeſted by this Court to continue in his government, the reſtoration of Cheyt Sing is neceſſarily given up; while at the ſame time, it may be proper on his part, to ſubmit to the reſtoration of Mr. Briſtow and Mr. Fowke— but while I ſay this, and declare it as my opinion, that in every controverſy between the Directors and the Governor General, the power of the Directors muſt be ſupreme. — I beg leave to remark on the other hand, that much diſcretion muſt neceſſarily be left with the Governor General, and a due deference to his rank and ſituation ought always to be obſerved. From the diſtance at which he is placed, many things may occur, which could not be known at the time of iſſuing the order — wherever it ſhall evidently appear, that ſuch circumſtances are material in determining on the point in iſſue, at the time of giving the orders, and which were not known to the Court of Directors, I ſhall not think the Governor General to blame in referring the matter again to their conſideration; but when, with all thoſe circumſtances before them, they have a ſecond time reſolved, their orders muſt be implicitly obeyed. In the ſame manner the Court of Directors muſt, by our conſtitution, ſubmit to the deciſion of a General Court — while the General Court ſhould always be careful and cautious not to violate the reſpect which is due to the perſons they have choſen for the management of their affairs — Thus in the caſe of Mr. Briſtow and Mr. Fowke; I think Mr. Haſtings was bound to place them in the ſituations, to which the Court of Directors had ordered them to proceed, at Oude and Benares. At the ſame time I am of opinion, that it was below the Court of Directors to make this a cauſe of difference with their chief Governor, who ſhould undoubtedly have the choice of the men he is to employ in confidential embaſſies to foreign powers. It is impoſſible the Court of Directors can be ſo good judges of the merits of their ſervants in this reſpect, as the Governor General on the ſpot. Even the nomination of Mr. Briſtow and Mr. Fowke, ſhew that they were not appointments in the ordinary line of ſuceſſion, becauſe many of their ſeniors might have claimed thoſe ſtations — ſuppoſing the Court of Directors had interfered in the appointment of Mr. Anderſon to negociate with Scindia, it is probable that no other man could have been found of equal ability; this ſhews Mr. Haſtings is not inattentive to merit in the objects of his selection: the politics of Oude and Benares are equally links in the chain of negotiation. It would be deemed extremely severe even in his Majesty, to insist upon appointing ambassadors to the courts of Europe, notoriously hostile to the ministry he employed; and yet there is no doubt of his Majesty's power to send any ambassadors he thinks proper. In every situation there are confidential places, which the Supreme power always leaves to the efficient person, who is to carry his orders into execution, to fill up as he pleases. The Admiralty has an undoubted right to appoint captains, but it is always left to a flag officer to name such a person as he approves, for the command of the ship where the flag is hoisted. The answer of Mr. Hastings was putting the controversy in a true light, "If you persist in ordering those gentlemen to confidential posts which have always hitherto been filled up by the Governor General, you ought to recall me; it is better that I should be removed, than the authority of your government be weakened in the eyes of the natives." In this there was nothing disrespectful, it was the language of a man who felt the dignity of his trust, and the interest of the public good. When Hannibal arrived in Afric to the relief of Carthage, the council sent him orders how he was to proceed in the manner of attacking Scipio. His answer was, "That in matters of civil concern, the council of Carthage must determine; but while they entrusted him with the command of their army, he must be left at liberty to judge how to attack the Romans.

Another

Another reaſon why I am anxious this queſtion ſhould paſs unanimouſly is, the effect it will neceſſarily have on his Majeſty's Miniſters. They will certainly be more cautious in proceeding to puniſh thoſe men who have received ſuch teſtimonies of public applauſe; at leaſt it will oblige them to examine true merit with their own eyes. Whatever prejudices they may have received from the repreſentations of the principal member of the Select Committee, I imagine when the approbation of ſo reſpectable a circle of Proprietors as are now aſſembled, they will deliberate twice before they proceed in the career he has pointed out. There was a time when the influence of that gentleman was ſuch, that his authority would have been ſufficient to have directed the reſolutions of his party without farther examination; but I believe this implicit influence no longer exiſts. If therefore our proceedings have no other effect than to enforce a ſtrict examination, I think we have gained a great deal; neither can I believe for my own part, that the Duke of Portland, and his friends the Cavendiſhes, noted as the Bourbons for good-nature, will bind themſelves to the reſentment of others, and join in the perſecution of a man who has rendered ſuch national ſervices; nor that they who formerly maintained the danger of violating chartered rights, will in the firſt ſeſſion of Parliament after getting into power, forget all the doctrines they have held on the ſubject reſpecting this very Company.

I there-

I therefore move, Sir, " That it is the opinion of this Court, that Warren Haſtings, Eſq. Governor General, and the other members of the Supreme Council, have diſplayed uncommon zeal, ability and exertion in the management of the affairs of the Eaſt-India Company during the late hoſtilities in India, particularly in ſupporting the war in the Carnatic, under ſo many preſſing difficulties, when that country was in danger of being loſt by the ſucceſsful irruption of Hyder Ally Cawn, aided by the French, and alſo for concluding the late treaty of peace with the Marattas, at a period ſo very critical, and on terms ſo honourable and advantageous to the permanent intereſts of the Company.

" Reſolved, therefore, That the thanks of this Court be given to Warren Haſtings, Eſq. and the other members of the Supreme Council, for the above ſpecified great and diſtinguiſhed ſervices; and that this Court doth requeſt the ſaid Warren Haſtings, Eſq. Governor General, not to reſign the ſtation he now holds, until the tranquillity of our poſſeſſions in India ſhall be reſtored, and the arrangements neceſſary upon the re-eſtabliſhment of peace ſhall have taken place."

Before I ſit down I hope the Court will indulge me in ſaying a few words on a ſubject, which I admit is ſomewhat extraneous to the preſent queſtion, while at the ſame time it naturally riſes from the occurrences I have mentioned in the debate.—The

ſubject

ſubject I allude to is the ſuſpenſion of General Matthews, after being inſtrumental in ſo glorious a degree to the conqueſt of Bednore and Mangalore. I am far from ſaying there may not be good cauſe for his ſuſpenſion; at the ſame time I declare, I am filled with every prejudice in his favour to induce me to think the contrary. I ſhall go farther, by ſaying that all the reaſons I have yet heard aſſigned in vindication of ſuch proceedings, fortifies me more and more in opinion, that they do not exiſt on any juſtifiable grounds.—This officer ſeems to me to have revived that ſpirit of irregular enterprize by which we acquired our poſſeſſions in the Eaſt Indies, and by which we muſt preſerve them.—It was more particularly applicable to the countries which he attacked where European armies had not before penetrated—The conduct of a General in ſuch proceedings can only be eſtimated by his ſucceſs. The ignorance of our adverſaries, the fear which our raſhneſs conveys to their mind, the enthuſiaſm the troops acquire in ſuch a career, are all to be eſtimated in the ſcale of our proceedings. Who can pretend to meaſure the conduct of Cortez by the ſcale of human prudence? We are told, that the cauſe of ſuperſeding General Matthews, is the ſtorming a number of forts which he might have marched round without loſing any of his troops; perhaps this was neceſſary both to intimidate the enemy and to encourage his own men, when they ſaw that ſuch fortifications could give no protection to the one, nor obſtruction to the other; perhaps a moment's delay in marching by detours would have hazarded the main enterprize; in ſhort, I can imagine a thouſand ſituations which would render ſuch a conduct commendable, inſtead of being liable to any blame. Another charge is, that General Matthews had marched to the capital of Bidnour (Hydernagur) without proviſions or any ammunition, and thereby riſqued the whole army. This alſo is vindicated by his ſucceſs. He took the province, and has ſince conquered Mangalore. There are hardly any accounts of our tranſactions in the Eaſt which are more ſplendid, or of more conſequence, or which happened at a time more critical; and yet this officer is ſuperſeded and diſgraced, upon the complaint of ſome of his Majeſty's officers who would have proſecuted the war according to the more eſtabliſhed rules of their profeſſion.—I wiſh to pay every deference to his Majeſty's officers; I wiſh to ſhow them every attention that does not diminiſh the ſpirit of the Company's troops. They are both in their ſeveral ſtations, officers of the State, which has thought an incorporated Company the beſt mode of governing thoſe poſſeſſions, whoſe profits can only be made beneficial by the means of commerce; but, whenever the ſpirit of that ſervice ſhall be broken, or ideas ſhall go forth, that a man, becauſe he holds his Majeſty's commiſſion is neceſſarily more knowing than a perſon under the authority given to the Company, though the one may have ſeen many years of ſervice, while the other can claim no conſideration from experience; I ſay, that in ſuch a ſtate of things, it were better to ſurrender the charter

at

at once than admit of ſuch maxims; and, therefore, as long as we hold the power, we muſt ſupport the perſons neceſſary for maintaining it, not in any partial conteſt between the King's troops and the Company's troops, but in an exact and equal diſtribution of juſtice on any diſpute that may ariſe between them; and this is all I ſhall ſay on ſubject at preſent, farther than adding, by way of recommendation, that no time may be loſt in rendering this juſtice to General Matthews.

When the Governor had finiſhed his ſpeech, the clerk read extracts from the public diſpatches, by which it appeared that the ſucceſſes of General Matthews had been moſt rapid and important: that he had taken Onore and Merghy, where he found a very conſiderable ſupply of naval ſtores belonging to Hyder Ally; and had burnt one ſixty-four gun ſhip, and two fifties, which were nearly compleated, beſides ſeveral ſmaller veſſels: that he afterwards entered the province of Bidnour, and took ſeveral forts—forced the paſſes to the capital, which ſurrendered to him upon terms in February laſt: and that Mangalore, the capital of Hyder's poſſeſſions on the Malabar coaſt, had ſince been taken by General Matthews. The clerk then read a letter from Mr. Anderſon to the Court of Directors, in which he ſtates that ſince the final ratification of the Maratta peace, he had made great progreſs in a ſeparate treaty of alliance with the Marattas againſt Tippoo Saib: and he next read an account of the retreat of Tippoo Saib ſrom the Carnatic, and that the Britiſh troops took poſſeſſion of Arcot on the 13th of March. The ſupplies ſent to Madras and Bombay ſince the commencement of the preſent war, by the Governor General and Council of Bengal, were, to Madras, about two hundred and ten lacks of rupees, and to Bombay, three hundred and thirty lacks, making above five hundred and forty lacks of rupees, or ſix millions ſterling. The accounts farther ſtated, that the troops in the province of Oude had been paid to a day, and that there was a very conſiderable increaſe in the revenues.

Mr. *Dallas* roſe to ſecond the motion, but was prevented by Mr. Edward Moore, who deſired to know if there were no other papers to read. He wiſhed to aſk the Chairman if he was not prepared with an anſwer to the very extraordinary letter which had been received from Mr. Haſtings; and he wondered that that letter had not been read. That letter contained a direct charge againſt the Directors. Mr. Moore was proceeding, when he was called to order by Governor Johnſtone, who ſaid, that as the advices had been open for the inſpection of the proprietors, he had not called for farther papers; and particularly that he thought there was no occaſion to call for that letter, as it had been read at the laſt General Court, and conſequently was before the proprietors; add to this, it had been printed in all the newſpapers: but that the honourable gentleman might undoubtedly

undoubtedly move for the reading of any paper he thought proper.

General *Ogletborpe* desired to speak to order. He said the Court had then a motion before them, which, as he understood, a learned gentleman was ready to second; afterwards the honourable and worthy gentleman might undoubtedly move for the production of any paper he thought proper: but the General begged they would proceed in order, and that Mr. Dallas should be permitted to second the motion then before the Court.

Mr. *Dallas* then rose, and seconded the motion, in words nearly to the following effect: —

Mr. Chairman,

I RISE to second the motion made by the honourable Governor; and in the discharge of a task, so grateful to my feelings, I shall have occasion to take up but little of the time of the Court; because I am sensible, that it is not in my power to throw additional light upon a subject which the honourable Governor has already placed in so striking a point of view; and besides, that I hope, this is a motion which will meet with no opposition. However much we may have differed upon former occasions, I trust that in the present instance the Court will have but one feeling, and one voice.

At the ſame time that I ſay this, I ſhould be extremely ſorry if the object of the preſent motion were to be the reſult of ſenſeleſs unanimity, or careleſs indifference. I feel that we are ſoliciting for Mr. Haſtings, what to a mind independent like his, and above mean and baſe conſiderations, muſt be the moſt valuable reward, the approbation of his conſtituents, publicly and honourably expreſſed. I am aware, however, that the thanks of bodies of men have, of late, been proſtituted to ſuch unworthy purpoſes, that they can ſcarcely be conſidered as conferring honour or diſtinction; and that a man of real merit may turn away with contempt from an offering, which the empty profeſſions of every artful impoſtor never fail to obtain from a credulous and deluded public. But the thanks for which we move this day, muſt be founded upon great and meritorious ſervices, of which undeniable evidence is upon your table; and I truſt, that they will be offered and accepted as the effuſion of real gratitude, and the genuine tribute of the heart.

Before I enter upon the conſideration of the preſent motion, I muſt be permitted to look back to what paſſed upon a former occaſion, I mean that memorable day, when the manly and ſpirited interpoſition of this Court reſcued Mr. Haſtings from unjuſt obloquy and unmerited puniſhment; and by continuing him in his preſent ſtation, in oppoſition to the vote of the Court of Directors, enabled him, as the honourable Governor has pointedly obſerved, to perform those services which, to-day, are the subject of public congratulation. At that period of time our affairs, at best, wore a doubtful aspect: we were engaged in a long and ruinous war, and had nothing but the assurances of Mr. Hastings, that peace would be soon restored. Opposed to these assurances were the confident declarations of men in high and responsible situations, that Mr. Hastings either deceived the Court of Proprietors, or was himself deceived upon the occasion. Yet upon a ballot, when notwithstanding, if there were no direct interference, yet the sense of administration was supposed to be hostile to Mr. Hastings; with the votes of the Directors in support of their own resolutions; with all their influence exerted among their friends and connections, and their authority exercised over their dependants; with all the disappointed men, and personal enemies, which the long possession of power can never fail to create: of upwards of twelve hundred Proprietors, only the miserable number of seventy-five could be collected together to vote for Mr. Hastings's removal. If such, at that time, were the support he received, will he be deserted, at the present day, by those whose assistance he then possessed; after he has brought our affairs to the most favourable issue; when hope is realized, and expectation fulfilled; and his conduct has completely justified the confidence reposed in him?

But if any opposition should arise to the present motion, I will state upon what grounds it appears to me me that oppoſition muſt reſt. The motion conſiſts of two diſtinct propoſitions: the firſt, A vote of thanks to Mr. Haſtings and the other members of the Supreme Council for ſpecified ſervices; the ſecond, A requeſt to Mr. Haſtings, not to reſign his preſent ſtation until the tranquillity of our poſſeſſions in India ſhall be reſtored, and the arrangements neceſſary upon the eſtabliſhment of peace ſhall have taken place. Whoever reſiſts the firſt part of the motion, muſt either Deny the exiſtence of the facts which it aſſerts, or affirm, That they are not of a nature to entitle Mr. Haſtings and the members of the Supreme Council to thanks: and with reſpect to the ſecond part, undoubtedly, evidence to ſhew, That though in theſe particular inſtances Mr. Haſtings has deſerved well of the Company, yet his general conduct has been of a nature to render ſuch a requeſt improper, will be ground, upon which, if juſt, it ought to be oppoſed with ſucceſs.

With regard to the relief of the Carnatic, it is a circumſtance of public notoriety, a particular account of which is upon the table, and therefore a fact which I ſhall treat as beyond denial. It remains only to be conſidered, whether, and in what degree, that relief was owing to the Governor General, and the Supreme Council of Bengal.

Of the ample and extraordinary ſupplies ſent from time to time by the government of Bengal for the relief of the Carnatic, the paper which was read ſome

time

time ago contains a detailed account, and affords irresistible evidence. These supplies have been furnished during a period of public distress, and when the enemies of Mr. Hastings were loud in their assertions, that the resources of Bengal were not equal to the exigencies of its own government. An impoverished country, an exhausted treasury, an army in arrear, the civil servants unpaid, it was confidently predicted, could terminate in nothing less than disaffection in the provinces, revolt in the troops, impotence in the hour of foreign attack, rebellion among the civil servants, in a word, in the ruin of the East India Company's affairs. Yet notwithstanding the internal distress of Bengal, a distress unavoidably occasioned by a long and expensive war, undertaken, as this court has already voted, in obedience to the positive commands of the Court of Directors, the exertions of that government enabled it to afford the relief you have heard stated, and to preserve, within itself, tranquillity and peace. I admit the distress of Bengal to have been great; but I contend, that in proportion to that distress is the merit of the Supreme Council, in affording supplies to the Carnatic, at a time when their own wants were of so pressing a nature. In addition to the evidence you have already heard, I will beg leave to add the testimony of those who were upon the spot, and whose situations render them competent witnesses upon the occasion. General Stuart, in a minute recorded upon the Madras consultations, begs leave to dissent from a paragraph contained in the general letter from that government to the Court of Directors, and which aſcribes our ſucceſs in the Carnatic to the good conduct of Lord Macartney, becauſe he is convinced that it is owing to the gallantry of Sir Eyre Coote, and the unparallelled exertions of Mr. Haſtings. Sir Eyre Coote himſelf, that great and gallant officer, who, with a handful of men, has triumphed over mighty nations, and achieved conqueſts, than which the page of hiſtory can afford none more brilliant, in a letter to the Supreme Council, imputes his ſucceſs to the liberal ſupport with which Mr. Haſtings had furniſhed him. And here, let me draw the attention of the Court to a fact which will ſtrongly enforce the propriety of the preſent motion. Sir Eyre Coote has received the thanks of the nation for the ſervices he has performed in the Carnatic. We have his own authority, that theſe ſervices were the conſequences of the liberal ſupplies he received from Mr. Haſtings. What then! Shall Sir Eyre Coote receive the thanks of his country for the ſervices he has performed, and ſhall they be denied to Mr. Haſtings, who enabled him to perform theſe ſervices?

Allowing to the other members of the Supreme Council all the praiſe that zeal and ability employed in the public ſervice deſerve, the honourable Governor has informed the court, that to Mr. Haſtings the relief of the Carnatic is moſt peculiarly to be aſcribed. One fact alone will place this truth beyond doubt, and above contradiction.

The

The firſt intelligence of the irruption of Hyder Ally into the Carnatic, was communicated to the Supreme Council at Bengal, with all thoſe circumſtances of diſtreſs and horror which attended it, at a period when their own reſources were in an exhauſted ſtate, and when the long prevalence of internal diſcord in the public Councils had relaxed all the ſprings of Government. Terror confounded, deſpair overwhelmed every ordinary mind. But the ſoul of Mr. Haſtings was incapable of diſpondence. The Council was aſſembled. With advice ſuited to the occaſion, he propoſed, by a vigorous and daring effort, to afford the government of Madras, their only chance of ſafety, and to ſend them an immediate ſupply of fifteen lacks of rupees, and a reinforcement of ſix hundred and thirty Europeans, with Sir Eyre Coote to head the army. Theſe troops were to be tranſported by ſea, at a ſeaſon of the year when the navigation was ſuppoſed to be impracticable, and had been unattempted even by the adventurous ſpirit of commerce. But what was the conduct of Mr. Francis upon the occaſion? Inſtead of propoſing any meaſures for the relief of the Carnatic, he trembled for the ſafety of Bengal. The project of Mr. Haſtings communicated freſh terrors to his breaſt. He objected to the ſupply of treaſure, becauſe it was impoſſible to foreſee how ſoon their own government might ſtand in need of it; and he oppoſed the reinforcement of troops, becauſe it was inconſiſtent with the ſafety of Fort William. Let us retire into the citadel and defend ourſelves, was the advice of Mr.

Francis. Let us march out, and attack the enemy upon the confines, was the cry of Mr. Haſtings. In what ſituation would the Company's affairs have been, had the prudent counſels of the former gentleman prevailed? If Sir Eyre Coote, with this actual ſupply in money and troops at the time, and with additional ſupplies poured in occaſionally, could barely ſtem the tide of battle, and maintain his ground, what would have been his fate had he arrived upon the coaſt, without treaſure and without troops, to head a diſpirited army, againſt an enemy confident from victory, and fluſhed with ſucceſs? Was not the honourable Governor warranted to aſſert, that the relief of the Carnatic is peculiarly owing to the ſpirited conduct of Mr. Haſtings?

If ſuch were the peculiar merit of Mr. Haſtings in the relief of the Carnatic, let us conſider whether he has an excluſive claim to praiſe for his conduct, with reſpect to the Maratta peace. The firſt and immediate cauſe of that peace is generally admitted to have been the attack upon Mahdajee Scindia's dominions; and I will now ſtate to the court the hiſtory of that attack.

A minute entered upon the public conſultations of the 12th of June, 1780, in the ſecret department, and ſigned by Mr. Haſtings, after ſtating, in general terms, the probable advantages of activity in bringing the Maratta war to a concluſion, contains the following propoſal: — *Let it be given in*

*inſtructions*

*instructions to Major Camac, if he shall find it practicable, to march his detachment, in conjunction with the forces, which the Ranna by his treaty will be obliged in such a case to furnish, directly to the capital of the territory dependent upon Mahdajee Scindia. This cannot fail to divert him from the war in Guzzerat; and by bringing it home to his own interests, which have hitherto been wholly exempted from it, induce him to be an equal solicitor for peace, to which at this time he appears to be the only impediment.* — Whoever, with the knowledge of what has since happened, shall read this minute of Mr. Hastings, and consider the actual state of affairs in India at the time, to him it will more resemble the spirit of prophecy, than the efforts of a human mind from causes deducing their effects. It seems as if his penetrating eye had pierced into futurity. Inspirited by the confidence of success, he concludes this minute with more than his ordinary warmth, and conjures his colleagues in the most pressing terms to concur with him in the measure, or, at least, if they cannot concur, to desist from opposing, and to leave to him all the responsibility, and the consequences attending it. At length, kindling into enthusiasm, he adds, Would to God I could be answerable with my life for the consequences! To those who are acquainted with the character of Mr. Hastings, this will not appear a vain-glorious boast; nor will they hesitate to believe that he would chearfully resign, at the public call, a life, of which three and thirty years have constituted a series of unremitted efforts for its service.

Such

Such was the minute which Mr. Haſtings deliver-ed in upon this occaſion. Succeſs, however, was not the conſequence; and Mr. Wheeler's name appeared to a minute, jointly with that of Mr. Francis, ſtating objections, and diſſenting from the meaſure. The enormous expence which would attend the expedition, was urged, among other reaſons, why it ought not to take place. And now, let me entreat the ſerious attention of thoſe who hear me to the conduct of Mr. Haſtings. In his anſwer given in to this minute, he obviates the objection of expence in a manner which will ſcarcely occur to any mind. I will quote, at length, the paſſage, for the honour of human nature — "As the expence which will attend the meaſure which I have recommended is the only formal objection made to it, I hope I may be allowed to remove it, by offering to exonerate the Company from it, and to take it upon myſelf. The contingencies of the detachment are the only expence that can reaſonably be charged to the expedition. Theſe I rate at far below two lacks of rupees.* That ſum I offer to contribute to this diſburſement. I have already depoſited it, within a ſmall amount, in the hands of the ſub-treaſurer; and I beg that the Board will permit it to be accepted for that ſervice." — Let the noiſy declaimers againſt eaſtern venality and corruption ſtand forward, and produce, from the annals of their own times, a ſimilar inſtance of zeal for the public ſervice! Let the barefaced pretenders to pa-

* £25,000 ſterling.

triotic virtue, who daily ſtun the nation with their impudent profeſſions, exhibit, in the ſtory of their own lives — not an offer of ſervice in this extent — but any thing that reſembles the principle which gave birth to it! Of the numerous volumes produced by the Select Committee, and devoted to the purpoſes of foul accuſation, could not one page be reſcued from its odious fate, and conſecrated to the recital of ſuch an inſtance of exalted virtue? Did conſcience draw ſelf-degrading compariſons? I forbear to enquire into the motives which occaſioned this ſilence — But this much I will venture to predict, Though thought unworthy to be regiſtered in the dignified productions of the Select Committee, it will live in the public memory, long after their authors ſhall be laid in duſt, and themſelves, and their productions, equally forgotten.

This minute had the misfortune to experience a like fate with the former, and only drew from Meſſrs. Francis and Wheeler a laboured reply, in which they perſiſt in their oppoſition. I admit that reply to abound in plauſible and ingenious argument; in ſubtle objections, and refined diſtinctions. Neither do I mean to inſinuate, that it did not proceed from the conſcientious exerciſe of their judgement. In truth, it was a project to ſtagger every ordinary mind. Even the honourable gentleman who makes this motion, and who is not apt to be confounded by the boldneſs of any ſcheme, has declared upon a former occaſion, it would have ſtartled him. But it is in the perilous conjuncture, and upon the desperate occasion, that the genius of Mr. Hastings asserts its superiority. While the gentlemen who opposed him were dismayed with the difficulties and dangers of this plan; alarmed at the distance of the expedition; terrified at its expence; with-holding the public treasure to provide for the last extremity; urging the possibility of an invasion of their own provinces, which would be left in a defenceless state: — Mr. Hastings felt that there were seasons when the public safety must be risked; and when upon the dangerous hazard of daring councils, depends the only remaining chance of success. — I turn away from the unhappy personal consequences, which afterwards followed from this minute, betwixt Mr. Hastings and Mr. Francis. — It is sufficient to say, the expedition at length took place. Every thing Mr. Hastings had predicted was verified in the event. *Mahdajee Scindia's camp was attacked with success; his attention was drawn off from the War in the Guzzerat to the defence of his own territories; he became a solicitor for peace*; and from the enemy whom we had most reason to dread, was converted into the friend in whom we had most cause to confide; and the faithful negociator, by whose interposition Mr. Hastings was enabled to accomplish the present peace.

In stating the minutes which passed upon this occasion, I hope it will not be imagined, that I mean any disrespect either to the name of Mr. Francis or Mr. Wheeler. I respect the abilities, and I regard the

integrity

integrity of Mr. Francis; but it is from the triumph over the oppoſition of ſuch abilities, that the character of Mr. Haſtings derives additional luſtre. With reſpect to Mr. Wheeler, Mr. Haſtings himſelf has borne the moſt honourable teſtimony to his private worth, and to his public merit.

Having ſtated, at ſome length, to the Court, the conduct of Mr. Haſtings, with reſpect to the attack upon Scindia's dominions, I have only one circumſtance more to mention, that regards this ſubject. The plan for a ſeparate peace with Scindia, after the ſucceſs of that attack, was dictated by Mr. Haſtings while upon the Benares expedition; ſubſequent to the aſſaſſination of the troops; all the horrors of that ſcene yet recent; the ground ſtill ſmoaking with the blood which had been ſhed; dangers encompaſſing his own perſon; a retreat to be effected with an inconſiderable eſcort through a country, which it was apprehended might riſe up in arms — at ſuch a time, diſregarding the dangers which ſurrounded him; his mind, calm and undaunted, was only employed upon projects for the public benefit; and he formed, and diſpatched to Colonel Muir, the plan of that ſeparate peace with Mahdajee Scindia, which has ſince conducted to a general pacification with all the Maratta powers. In the progreſs of the negotiation he had every difficulty to encounter. The moſt violent oppoſition upon the ſpot, was countenanced by the ſupport of the Court of Directors at home. The language which iſſued from this country, was of a nature to dispirit Mr. Hastings, and render those, with whom he had to treat, imperious and impracticable. The necessity of peace was stated in the most abject terms, and the deplorable sentiments entertained by those, who had the management of the Company's affairs, were circulated with active zeal through all the nations of Indostan. Censures were aimed, and threats denounced against Mr. Hastings. Every method was pursued to counter act his efforts, by lessening his personal weight and consequence. Yet under all these circumstances, without friends, and without support, obnoxious to the resentment of the Court of Directors, and conducting a war, the unavoidable expence of which had rendered it unpopular to the nation; he has manifested through every part of this arduous negotiation, a firmness of mind which no circumstances could shake; a spirit proof against the contagion of fear; and instead of suffering his conduct to be influenced by the opposition he received, he has acted with the same confidence, as if he had been backed with all the support the country could afford. *Not to have despaired of the Commonwealth*, was, in Roman times, a subject for public thanks. What praise then is due to him, by whose spirited conduct, through a long season of general despondence, we have at length obtained a most honourable and advantageous peace!

You all remember how confident were the predictions of Mr. Hastings's enemies, that the assurances of this peace were delusive and deceitful; with what

what contemptuous ſneers they treated our weak credulity, and ridiculed a belief which could only be occaſioned by the moſt profound ignorance. Theſe predictions muſt either have been the effect of intereſted malice, or of conſcientious belief. In the firſt caſe, it is in vain to urge the advantages of the preſent peace; for that malice will not be leſs inveterate, becauſe covered with ſhame; but in the latter, Mr. Haſtings muſt receive all the commendation liberal minds can beſtow. Such aſſertions were acknowledgments of the difficulties which ſtood in the way of a peace; and muſt now become teſtimonies to the merit of the man whoſe unparallelled exertions have removed theſe difficulties. What will they ſay who predicted *no* peace, to *ſuch* a peace? It ſeems the characteriſtic of Mr. Haſtings, not only to refute the malicious prognoſtics of his enemies, but to outdo the moſt extravagant predictions of his friends.

I have now, Sir, troubled the Court, very much at length, upon the former part of this motion; and I flatter myſelf no doubts remain, that the conduct of Mr. Haſtings, and the other members of the Supreme Council, is entitled to our thanks, in the two inſtances of the relief of the Carnatic, and of the Maratta peace. I have a few words to add with reſpect to the latter part of the motion, The requeſt to Mr. Haſtings not to reſign his government at the preſent period.

I have ſaid, that if evidence can be produced to ſhew, That the general conduct of Mr. Haſtings has been of a nature to render ſuch a requeſt improper, this part of the motion ought to be oppoſed with ſucceſs. What has been that general conduct?

The honourable gentleman who made the motion has already adverted to a report prepared by a committee of the Houſe of Commons, and which contains ſerious accuſations againſt the conduct of Mr. Haſtings. I rejoice that the honourable Governor has introduced this ſubject, becauſe this is an occaſion upon which it would have been unfair not to have adverted to a circumſtance of ſuch a nature, and beſides, that the enemies of Mr. Haſtings have circulated this report, during the receſs, with the moſt malevolent aſſiduity, as a publication which, they flatter themſelves, will prove deſtructive to his fame. It falls within my own experience that this publication has undoubtedly left impreſſions unfavourable to Mr. Haſtings upon honourable and impartial minds; and it is become incumbent upon his friends to prevent, as far as may be in their power, theſe prejudices from affecting the public opinion. It is true, that ſubſequent to that report having been preſented to the Houſe, the intelligence arrived of the Maratta peace; a ſervice of ſo brilliant a nature, that the honourable Governor flatters himſelf, it will not only ſhield Mr. Haſtings from all farther proſecution, but that thoſe who have been moſt vehement in his cenſure, will become

moſt

moſt earneſt in his praiſe. With his political experience, and ſound knowledge of mankind, can the honourable gentleman ſeriouſly entertain ſuch hopes? If great and meritorious ſervices, if unblemiſhed integrity, if virtuous conſiſtency of conduct, could have diſarmed his enemies, would Mr. Haſtings have endured the perſecution he has already undergone? It is, as the honourable Governor has truly ſtated it to be, A ſtruggle for power; and the ardour of thoſe engaged in it will only encreaſe from what has happened; their efforts will be violent in proportion as their ſituation is become deſperate. Againſt theſe efforts it becomes us to provide, and to afford Mr. Haſtings a ſupport, as honourable to ourſelves, as I hope it will prove beneficial to him.

An honourable gentleman (Mr. Moore) behind me, was very anxious, ſome time ſince, that a letter, dated the 20th of March, 1783, and addreſſed by Mr. Haſtings to the Court of Directors, ſhould be read to the court, and he charged the honourable Governor with partiality in having moved that ſuch papers only might be read as would conduce to the purpoſe of his motion, and holding back from the public view thoſe which might juſtify an oppoſition to it. Having made this attack upon the conduct of another, the honourable gentleman will permit me to enquire how far his own will ſtand examination. In anſwer to a queſtion put to him by the honourable Governor, the worthy Proprietor declared, that he had not read the Maratta treaty, the chief paper

in

in ſupport of this motion, and which, one would imagine, not merely thoſe immediately intereſted, but every man not totally indifferent to public events, would have attentively conſidered. But yet, though this paper be ſo material to his information, and I take leave to add, indiſpenſable to his fair deciſion upon the ſubject, the honourable gentleman never moves for it, though it has not been read, but calls for another paper, which he thinks will criminate Mr. Haſtings. If he wiſhed for full information, he was equally bound to move for one paper as for the other; but if not to move for every paper be a proof of partiality, in the ſame ſentence in which he has urged the accuſation againſt another, he has incurred the guilt of it himſelf. Which be the moſt venial offence, a partiality to acquit, or a partiality to condemn? let the Court determine. Thus much with reſpect to the honourable gentleman's impartiality, and the temper with which he comes to the diſcuſſion of this queſtion. But, in truth, there is no foundation for the charge which he has preferred. With regard to the letter which he has mentioned, I myſelf would have ſeconded his motion, if I had not entertained too much regard for the time of the Court, to trouble them with the long reading of a paper, read, as the honourable Governor has ſtated, at a former Court, and inſerted in all the public prints. While ſublimity of thought, while dignity of ſentiment, and magnanimity of ſoul, can command admiration, this letter of Mr. Haſtings will ſtand in the foremoſt rank of the compofitions of the human mind. It is true, it does contain accufation againft the Court of Directors, and that accufation ftated in terms of reproach; but dictated by a generous abhorrence of crimes with which he ftood falfely accufed. It is the tone of infulted honour; it is the language of injured virtue. Inftead of kneeling to unmerited cenfures, and crouching to the menacing arm of power, Mr. Haftings, with the boldnefs of confcious innocence, turns upon his accufers. Why did not the honourable gentleman call for the minute of the 14th of November, 1782, as a frefh proof of the haughty and imperious fpirit of Mr. Haftings? In that minute, after ftating the unhappy effects which muft neceffarily refult from the adminiftration of a man, deprived of public confidence, and ftripped of all fupport, he dictates to the Court of Directors a fpirited line of conduct, and conjures them immediately to confirm or recal him. He enforces the neceffity of coming to fome inftant refolution, for that either part of the alternative is fafety, when compared with the mifchiefs which muft refult from an unfettled government.

Thefe were fentiments fuited to the bold and manly fpirit of the right honourable Secretary of State (Mr. Fox;) and immediately upon the receipt of this minute, he declared in the Houfe of Commons, that whoever had read the laft difpatches from India, muft be convinced of the abfolute neceffity, that fomething fhould immediately be done.

A fhort

A ſhort time afterwards he informed the Houſe, that nothing but reaſons of neceſſity could juſtify delay in the buſineſs; that ſuch reaſ.ns exiſted; and among others, the Select Committee, he underſtood, had prepared a report, big with material information upon the ſubject, and neceſſary to enable the Houſe to determine wiſely upon the occaſion. In ſo urgent a conjuncture, the world will naturally expect that report to contain nothing but material information; and if it ſhall appear to have been delayed till near the riſing of the Houſe, from the inveſtigation of frivolous charges, and the inſertion of unimportant matter, whoever has thus delayed it, has trifled with the ſecurity of the Britiſh poſſeſſions in India. But if farther it ſhall be evident, that the aim of this report is more the deſtruction of an individual, than the advancement of the public good; be the author of it whom he may, he is a traitor to his truſt.

This report, big with the fate of India, has at length appeared; and I will venture to ſay, it is a production different, in its nature, from any which have preceded it. The world has hitherto been accuſtomed to conſider a Committee of the Houſe of Commons, as in the nature of a Court of Juſtice; the members of which, though bound by no religious tie, are under the moſt ſacred moral obligations to diveſt themſelves, as far as poſſible, of every corrupt view, partiality, and reſentment; to enquire temperately, and report diſpaſſionately. How far this

this duty has been obſerved in the preſent inſtance, the world will determine. It is the firſt report of a Committee of the Houſe of Commons, (and I appeal to the Journals of the Houſe, and to the experience of every man converſant with parliamentary buſineſs) in which ridicule, irony, and invective, are made uſe of as the means to criminate individuals, and perſuade the Houſe. A practice of ſo unjuſtifiable a nature, will, I truſt, produce no other effect than to alarm thoſe who are ultimately to decide; and will draw their attention to a more ſtrict examination of the evidence, when they have diſcovered the temper with which the report is prepared. In this examination, I aſſert in the face of the world, they will detect inſinuation without ground; aſſertion without proof; facts without evidence; language unwarrantably conſtrued; unjuſt inferences; and unfair concluſions. Theſe are bold accuſations, and I do not expect credit for them. I am not entitled to it. In every caſe the impartial mind muſt be determined by the greater degree of probability; and I confeſs it is infinitely more probable that I, from miſconception, from officious zeal, from blind attachment, or, if you pleaſe, from unworthy motives, ſhould prefer ſuch charges, than that a right honourable gentleman ſhould prepare, and a Committee of the Houſe of Commons approve, a report ſubject to them. But I throw out this warning to the world in the name of an abſent man. The only effect I wiſh to produce by it is, that whoever ſhall read the charges contained in this report, may likewiſe read the evidence in ſupport of them; and that no man who has not done this, will form an opinion upon the report unfavourable to Mr. Haſtings. This requeſt I am entitled to obtain, not merely on account of the aſſertions I have made, but becauſe it is reaſonable in itſelf; and I make it the more earneſtly, from the certain knowledge, that many minds have already been prejudiced by reading the report without a reference to the evidence. Let them be compared with each other, and the character of Mr. Haſtings will ſuſtain no injury. The poiſon and the antidote will be taken in together.

But, after all, what does this black catalogue contain? Stale accuſations, and exploded charges. Nine years have elapſed from the date of moſt of theſe ſuppoſed offences. The affair of Meſſrs. Briſtow and Fowke is once more revived. The reſignation by Mr. Macleane is renewed with every circumſtance of aggravation. The charge of corruption made in times of the greateſt political virulence, of which the acrimony of contention could explore no proof, and which was afterwards abandoned by thoſe who had preferred it, is again attempted, and held forth to public view. No tale is too improbable; no teſtimony too baſe. Even the gibbet muſt produce an evidence againſt him, and the infamous name of Nuncomar once more offend the ſight. The honourable Governor has particularly adverted to the charge of the Opium contract given to Mr. Sulivan. This contract was held by Mr. Sulivan upon the ſame

terms

terms it had been possessed by other persons, and this was the manner in which (while General Clavering and Mr. Francis sat at the Supreme Board) those terms were settled. It was put up to public advertisement, and of twelve competitors, bestowed upon him who offered the lowest terms. But Mr. Sullivan was the son of a gentleman who had eight times filled the Chair of the India Company, the private friend, and the public supporter of Mr. Hastings, and the aim of the charge is, that it was given as a means of future influence, or as the reward of past attachment, to a gentleman whose situation in the service did not entitle him to it. I will admit the full effect of the charge, and abandon Mr. Hastings to the censure which he merits upon the occasion. It was reserved for the accuser of Mr. Hastings to exhibit, upon his accession to power, splendid instances of disinterestedness and self-denial; to resist the claims of kindred and of blood, in favour of those who had claims upon the public! But these are not the feelings of common men. Mr. Hastings is a common man! subject to all the frailties and infirmities of human nature; to the impulse of friendship where it may be indulged without material detriment to the public service; to the feelings of gratitude, where public duty does not rigorously forbid him to give way to them. Indeed, indeed, these are pitiful accusations! If the character of Mr. Hastings is not of a sufficient polish to cast off such stains as these, it is time the right honourable gentleman's purposes should be fulfilled, and Mr. Hastings recalled. Which of these charges might not have been, with safety, deferred, till Mr. Hastings was upon the spot to explain his own conduct? If it be said that a scrutiny into that conduct was necessary to confirm or recal him, and that the safety of the British possessions in India materially depended upon the alternative, I answer, That the great charges of violation of treaties, of breach of national faith, of oppression of the native princes — any one of these charges, if true, was a a sufficient ground for his recal, and to enter into the consideration of the others was superfluous; if none of these charges were true, the others could only weigh as dust in the scale against him.

But, at least, this rigid scrutiny will prove the temper in which his conduct is investigated. With what feelings will the House receive so many volumes devoted to crimination; in which every trifling fault is blazoned in the most glaring colours, while a veil is cast over his merits and his services, and virtues which have won the respect, and secured him the esteem of mankind, are passed over in profound silence, and treated with utter neglect. The world have now evidence before them to determine, how far that honourable gentleman was right, who declared, That though a member of the Select Committee, he had not attended their meetings, because he had early discovered such symptoms of prejudice and party-spirit, that he was convinced their proceedings must terminate in injustice.

In what I have ſaid upon this ſubject, it has not been my intention to enter into an inveſtigation of the charges themſelves, becauſe I feel this is not the proper time, but to obviate the prejudices which the enemies of Mr. Haſtings have been induſtrious to excite. The day of trial muſt come, when the Houſe muſt either expreſs their diſapprobation of theſe charges, or ſuffer Mr. Haſtings to vindicate his character. The terms of Oppreſſor and public Robber muſt be retracted or proved. The right honourable gentleman ſtands pledged, in the face of God and his country, to prove Mr. Haſtings, The moſt notorious delinquent that ever exiſted in India. I truſt he has too much honour to conſider his exalted ſtation, as an eminence, from which, himſelf ſafe, and beyond reach, he may ſhower down upon the heads of others the deſtructive weapons of detraction and calumny. He will afford Mr. Haſtings an opportunity to meet his charge. But if unfortunately I ſhould prove miſtaken, the Houſe has too much honour, the Nation has too much juſtice, to endure ſuch conduct. Yes, the day muſt come, when the Governor General ſhall meet the right honourable gentleman in the face of God and of his country. To that day his friends look forward with eager hope. He himſelf has deſired to reſt the iſſue upon the moſt manly and ſpirited alternative, Reſtore me my Honour, or, Deprive me of my Life. His letter to the Court of Directors contains language to this effect, I am not guilty of the crimes which you have laid to my charge; but if I am, Away with your cold

and

and pitiful cenſures, I deſerve to die. This is the language of a man. In the mean time, let the world determine, Whether it is moſt probable, that they have preferred a falſe accuſation, who to offences of ſuch magnitude aſſign ſo inadequate a puniſhment, or that he is innocent of them, who entertains ſuch an abhorrence of the accuſation, that he diſclaims, in caſe he ſhall be found guilty, the lenity they would ſhew, and challenges the utmoſt puniſhment which human vengeance can inflict.

I fear, Sir, I have taken up a great deal too much of your time, upon a ſubject which the abilities of the honourable gentleman who made the motion had nearly exhauſted. It is unneceſſary for me to add, after the ſentiments I have profeſſed, that every part of the motion has my moſt hearty concurrence. The requeſt to Mr. Haſtings to continue in Bengal until the arrangements neceſſary upon the eſtabliſhment of peace ſhall have taken place, is no leſs founded in advantage to ourſelves than in gratitude to him. Three and thirty years of his life have paſſed away in the Company's ſervice. The experience of ſo long a period is an advantage which he muſt poſſeſs over every competitor. At an early age, his great abilities attracted the notice of Lord Clive, who appointed him Reſident at the Durbar, a ſtation, in which, it is generally known, he might have accumulated immenſe wealth. Yet after ſixteen years of ſervice he returned to England with a fortune ſo moderate, that he was obliged to go back to India, and went out with the appointment of ſecond in Council at Madras: a ſufficient proof of his great integrity. The knowledge of his abilities, and the opinion of his virtue, induced the Court of Directors to appoint him, while in this ſtation, to ſucceed to the Government of Bengal. Twelve years have paſſed ſince he has filled this arduous ſtation; not in times of tranquillity and eaſe, but of turbulence and diſtraction. He has not, indeed, as the honourable Governor obſerved, repoſed upon a bed of down; but (the honourable Governor will permit me to add) upon a pillow induſtriouſly planted with thorns. And ſhall we not ſupport him now that times more fortunate are arrived? Previous to the commencement of the oppoſition in Bengal, and during the two firſt years of his government, he had made material improvements in the internal adminiſtration of the Provinces entruſted to his care, and had in ſeveral inſtances received the commendatian of the Court of Directors. Now that peace is returned, and that unanimity prevails, he will purſue thoſe improvements to their utmoſt pitch of advantage. Poſſeſſing ſo many requiſites which can concur in no other man, to make the neceſſary eſtabliſhments upon the return of peace, and to ſettle the Government upon a permanent baſis, there is every reaſon to hope his plans will be founded in wiſdom, and productive of material benefit; and that he may be enabled to purſue this deſirable work, I moſt ſincerely ſecond the honourable gentleman's motion.

Mr.

Mr. *More* repeated his question.

Sir *Henry Fletcher* observed, that the letter of Mr. Hastings to the Court of Directors had been published in all the papers, and undoubtedly it contained charges which required that the Directors should enquire into the grounds of their conduct, and see if they could not justify it. He had done so — he had most carefully examined the records, and he had submitted the result to the Court of Directors, which was, in his own mind, a complete justification of their conduct. He certainly was at one time of opinion that peace would not have been made with the Marattas, for this reason; three distinct and contradictory negociations were opened — General Goddard sent Captain Watherston to the Court of Poona; another negociation was opened with the Rajah of Berar; and the third with Madajee Scindia. But on the death of Hyder Ally, and the conclusion of the war between England and France, he foresaw that the peace with the Marattas would be concluded — he said it at the time — and therefore the Marratta peace was not solely to be ascribed to the talents of Mr. Hastings, a part of the business must be allowed to the concatenation of events.

But to the question before the Court — In his mind it would be wise and temparate to enquire into the grounds of merit before they gave praise. To praise first, and to enquire into the propriety of do-

 ing

ing so afterwards, was neither dignified in the Court, nor honourable to the Governor General. Now there were certain points that must be enquired into — points which were not only very questionable, but ominous. For instance, by a resolution of the Council of Bengal, it appears on the records, that it was determined to give to Madajee Scindia one half of the city and territory of Broach. The offer of one half of it was made to him — but after the conclusion of the treaty with the Marattas, the whole was given up to him in a present without any reason being assigned, without any claim being made, without a single word being said to justify or explain the matter.

Broach produced a revenue, according to the last valuation at Bombay, sixteen lacks of rupees, which is two hundred thousand pounds. Thus hath the Governor General paid the enormous price of two hundred thousand pounds a year for this boasted peace with the Marattas. This was not all; on the very morning that the treaty was ratified, a private treaty was signed between Scindia and the Minister of the Marattas with so much secresy, that Mr. Anderson has not been able to come to the knowledge of it; and it was therefore a reasonable conclusion, that an engagement, made in so questionable a shape, was hostile to the Company. In addition to this, the Court of Directors had received a letter from Mr. Hornby, informing them, that since the treaty with the Marattas, one of our ships, on board of which were two officers of rank, who were going to an important command, was taken, and the officers were forcibly detained. Did this bear the aſpect of a cordial peace? And would it not be proper to enquire into thoſe particulars, before they come to the reſolution of thanks propoſed by the honourable Commodore? Sir Henry replied to ſeveral other of the matters thrown out; and in particular, he ſaid, that againſt two of the officers choſen and appointed by Mr. Haſtings, ſuch charges were exhibited, that they were ordered to Calcutta to explain their conduct.

Mr. *Sulivan.*

I CANNOT ſuffer what has fallen from the Chairman to paſs without a reply from behind the bar, leaſt it ſhould be ſuppoſed he has uttered the ſentiments of the Court of Directors. I am ſorry to ſee Mr. Haſtings treated ſo ungenerouſly. Surely it is a Chairman's duty to act impartially; but, inſtead of that, Sir Henry has not produced one inſtance out of a thouſand of Mr. Haſtings's great merits. Nothing but laboured invectives and groſs miſrepreſentations againſt the Governor General. For my own part, I revere the memory of thoſe immortal heroes, (turning to the ſtatues of Clive and Lawrence) although one of them was my inveterate enemy; but have they done more ſervice to the Company than Mr. Haſtings? What was the ſituation of the Company's pany's affairs when Mr. Haſtings ſucceeded to the government of Bengal in 1772? We were on the eve of a bankruptcy; and by the year 1775 he had encreaſed your property three millions eight hundred and thirty-nine thouſand pounds. What has he received in return? Not even thanks! And lately, when by a plan entirely his own, he has produced you a revenue of ſix hundred thouſand pounds a year, your Directors are ſilent, and actually blame him for appointing two or three extra men, who are to collect the duties which are paid into your coffers. Of what conſequence is it whether Mr. Haſtings employs three, or thirty-three negociators, when he has brought the treaty to a concluſion. I am aſhamed to reply to ſo frivolous a remark. The Chairman tells you he doubts the permanency of the peace, becauſe a ſecret article has been ſigned by the Marattas and Sindia, on the day the peace was ratified; yet you have intelligence from Mr. Anderſon, of a later date by a month, in which he ſpeaks confidently of the good faith of Sindia, and the Peſhwa; and that he has made great progreſs in a treaty of alliance with the Peſhwa and Sindia, againſt Tippoo Saib. I beg the Court will conſider from what quarter the Chairman receives his intelligence, and then they will conceive this to be as defective as that which he before received from Bombay. When the Fox packet arrived, which brought accounts that the ratified treaty was received in Sindia's camp, the Chairman brought a letter to us from an officer in Colonel Morgan's camp to Mr. Gregory, dated the 2d of laſt April. This mentioned that a large body of Marattas were preparing to enter the Guzzerat, and to attack Surat. At another time, when Mr. Haſtings wrote, that he was poſitive the peace with the Marattas would be concluded, if it was not ſo at that moment, our worthy Chairman damped our hopes by producing a letter from Bombay, ſaying that all hopes of peace were at an end; and that a large body of Marattas were preparing to enter the Concan. I would be glad to know what became of theſe great armies that were to invade the Concan and the Guzzerat? We have never heard a ſyllable more about them. I declare I am fully warranted, from what has happened, to with-hold my belief of any intelligence tranſmitted from Bombay, except the Governor and Council will vouch for the truth of the facts. But every idle tale of armies aſſembled, officers taken, no proſpect of peace, &c. &c. that we have hitherto received from private letters, ſent from ignorant natives in different parts of the Malabar coaſt, has turned out untrue. No wonder, however, that ſuch reports gained credit from thoſe, who, by their own letter to Bengal, expreſs a hope that the death of Hyder will make an alteration in the Maratta treaty, if not then ratified at Poona: and no wonder that the Bombay government catches hold of every ground, however ſlight, by which they expect to be able to retain their conqueſts. Such conduct is natural; and no wonder, Mr. Chairman, that thoſe gentlemen in this country, who are adverſe to Mr. Haſtings, adopt greedily, for facts, every report that tends

tends to diminish the lustre of that great man's character. With respect to Mr. Hastings, I avow, with pleasure, my friendship for him; — I think him the best servant the Company ever had, and that we owe our salvation to his wonderful and unparallelled exertions: — I have not a doubt that he will explain fully and satisfactorily his reasons for giving up Broach to Madajee Sindia: and so far from producing the Company sixteen lacks of rupees annually, I totally deny that it has ever produced them six, or any thing like it; and I am convinced it was a wise measure to cede it altogether.

Major *Scott*.

Sir HENRY FLETCHER,

I RISE to offer a few observations upon what you have been pleased to state to the Court; but before I proceed, I must beg leave to clear up a point which the Proprietors may misconstrue, if it is not now explained. You were pleased to observe, Sir, that Mr. Hastings had been mistaken in his judgment of two gentlemen whom he had patronized, in opposition to the orders of the Court of Directors. It might possibly be inferred, that Mr. Markham was one of those whose conduct Mr. Hastings had disapproved of: I hope I may be permitted therefore, in justice to the character of Mr. Markham, whom I am proud to call my friend, to declare, that Mr. Hastings has invariably mentioned that gentleman in terms of the greatest

greatest regard, and has particularly praised him for his abilities, the pointed attention he has paid to his orders, and to the duties of his station, while resident at Benares. It is true he has removed Mr. Middleton; and here, Sir, I think every candid man will allow, that the conduct of Mr. Hastings appears in the fairest point of view. Mr. Middleton was the person of his own choice in 1773. He continued resident at the court of Sujah Dowlah, till the majority of the Supreme Council removed him. He was again sent up to Oude, at the death of Colonel Monson, and was lately recalled, because Mr. Hastings thought he had not exerted himself as he might have done in the service of the Company. Surely, Sir, this is as strong an instance as can be given, that Mr. Hastings is not swayed by personal friendship, or any improper motives in his support of gentlemen in public stations. You have said, too, that you had long entertained doubts of the Maratta peace being effected, because Mr. Hastings had employed three negociators; one at Poona, Captain Watherston; another at Naigpoor, Mr. Chapman; and a third at the court of Sindia, Mr. Anderson. It is clear, however, that Mr. Hastings thought three negociators at least one too many, for he recalled Captain Watherston at the very time that he sent those instructions in a quill to Colonel Muir, which brought about a peace with Sindia. They were dispatched from Chunar, when his own person was in danger, and encompassed by the troops of Cheyt Sing. It does not appear, Sir, that the deputation of Mr.

Chapman

Chapman to Moodagee Boosla, impeded the negociation of Mr. Anderson; on the contrary, it was of material service. Peace with the Marattas was the object to be attained; it might possibly have been accomplished at Naigpoor, had it failed with Madajee Sindia. You have said too, that latterly, indeed, you did expect peace would be concluded with the Marattas, on account of the death of Hyder Ally, and the general peace in Europe. You added too, that you had submitted your sentiments to the Directors upon it some time ago; but what was the period when you did submit these sentiments to the Directors? Was it not after the arrival of the Fox packet? And did not that packet bring an account that the peace was ratified at Poona the 20th of December, arrived in Sindia's camp the 14th of January, and was to be interchanged the first fortunate day? To be sure, Sir, it was a proof of superior sagacity, to foretel that the peace, under such circumstances, would take place. If the paragraphs were dated prior to the Fox's arrival, why were they brought forward at all, when, by the intelligence then received, you knew that our affairs were so materially altered? I thought this mode of proceeding was peculiar to the Select Committee. There was not the most distant idea in India of a peace in Europe, when the treaty was ratified on the 20th of December, nor even when the last accounts left Bengal; and as Hyder died on the 7th, it was barely possible that intelligence of his decease should have reached Poona before the ratification of the treaty. Be that however

however as it may, hostilities with the Marattas had ceased eighteen months, owing to the separate treaty with Sindia, and the merit of that treaty solely and exclusively belongs to Mr. Hastings. You have observed too, that Mr. Hastings ceded to Sindia a territory producing sixteen lacks of rupees a year, and as a proof, you bring an estimate of the revenues of Broach. But though I am not versed in matters of revenue myself, yet my honourable friend behind me, (Mr. Baber) who perfectly understands the subject, will tell you, that it is from actual receipts, and not from estimates, that we must count our gains. If, Sir, you place against the receipts of the last year, the expence of the civil and military establishments necessary for its defence, I imagine you will find that Broach, instead of sixteen lacks, has not yielded you a nett profit of sixteen thousand rupees. Do you recollect that the Poona Committee engaged the faith of the Company for the cession of Broach to Sindia? And that although the Supreme Council denied the Company could possibly be bound by an irregular act, yet that Sindia, having saved our army, was entitled to particular attention from us. In consideration of the engagement entered into by the Poona Committee, and the services since performed by Sindia, the Supreme Council have entirely ceded Broach to him; and by so doing I think they have acted wisely; for the half of Broach, in our possession, the other half in the possession of the Marattas, collections of each party being frequently in the ſame village, I am clear we could not have kept one-half of the diſtrict, without involving the Company in a future war. I entirely adopt Mr. Francis's ſentiments on this ſubject, who has invariably oppoſed the acquiſition of detached territories on the Malabar coaſt, becauſe the revenues never can pay the expence of collecting them, and tend to involve us in conſtant diſputes with the Marattas. With reſpect to the ſecret articles, I do not know the intelligence on which your knowledge of the fact is grounded; but this I know, that Mr. Anderſon writes with the utmoſt confidence as to the ſincerity of the Marattas; and I will pay more attention to him than to looſe, imperfect information from Bombay, which has ſo often, and ſo fatally deceived us already. You ſeem to expreſs your doubts, Mr. Chairman, of the validity of the peace, becauſe two officers, who were on their way to Mangalore, were taken in a ſmall veſſel by the Marattas; but I deſire to bring to your recollection, Sir, that a ſhip, called the Aurora, was wrecked upon the Malabar coaſt, ſoon after the ſigning of Colonel Upton's treaty in March 1776, and though one article of that treaty was, that the cargoes of ſhips ſo wrecked ſhould be reſtored; no ſatisfaction whatever was received, and the Marattas declared that they could not controul the piratical free-booters who infeſted their coaſts: a fact we all know. You will find, I dare ſay, Sir, that thoſe officers and their property have been reſtored long ago, and ample ſatisfaction given for their captures, ſuppoſing they really were taken, for the intelligence is not poſitive.

I now come, Sir, to the revolution of Benares, and as the honourable and worthy gentleman, Mr. Moore, has called for your obſervations upon Mr. Haſtings's letter, I muſt beg leave to ſtate a few facts, which perhaps are not generally known to the proprietors. The revolution of Benares was, as you well know, Sir, eagerly ſeized hold of by the Select Committee in the month of April 1782, when a very imperfect account of the tranſaction was received in England. In the ſecond report the committee ſay, " that Cheyt Sing was patronized by us, in conſequence of ſervices rendered to our nation by his father." I have ſearched with all the induſtry I am capable of, but have not yet been able to find of what nature theſe ſervices were; but I do find from the following extracts from the records of the Eaſt-India Company, that the governor and council had ſeriouſly determined to diſpoſſeſs Bulwant Sing, the father of the late Rajah, of his country. The Governor and Council, in their inſtructions to Major Monro, dated the 6th of November, 1764, ſays, " With reſpect to Bulwant Sing, the double part he acted in the beginning of the war, ſufficiently warns us, to put no confidence in him; and, therefore, if he has not already been permitted to join you, or you have entered into no engagements with him, we would have him diſpoſſeſſed of his country, and his perſon, if poſſible, ſecured." April 1, 1765. " This man acted from the firſt ſo

wavering

wavering a part, that we wished to have no connection with him; but rather that his person should be secured, and some other placed in his Zemindary, who was more to be relied on; but Major Monro having committed him to a treaty, we consented to abide by it. In this also he failed; and therefore it was our intention to have trusted him no farther, which sentiment is expressed by the General in his letter from Cossinbuzar, where he points him out as one by no means to be depended upon. After Bulwant Sing had deserted our army, in violation of the treaty, it was our wish, that the country had been placed in the hands of some person in whose fidelity we might have had some dependence, and whose troops might have been an addition to our strength, in case of a renewal of the war; but as he had been again received on the faith of promises, though we wish none had been made till our sentiments were known, we shall abide by them."

As Bulwant Sing was situated between two powerful states, his indecisive and treacherous conduct is not to be wondered at; but I mention it, in contradiction to the report of the Select Committee, which states, that he had performed services to our nation, without specifying what those services were. They must have been considerable, to have counterbalanced the instances of insincerity and disaffection which I have mentioned.—The late Lord Clive thought it, however, consistent with true policy to protect Bulwant Sing from the vengeance of his old maſter Sujah Dowlah, who was compelled by the treaty of Allahabad, to continue him in the poſſeſſion of the Zemindaries of Benares and Ghauzipore. When Bulwant Sing died in 1770, our government interfered in the behalf of Cheyt Sing, his father's favourite, though, as Capt. Harper obſerved at that time, he was not, according to the Hindoo Laws, the lineal heir, being born by a woman of a low caſt, and he was in fact confirmed in poſſeſſion of the Zemindary in violation of the right of the preſent poſſeſſor, ſuppoſing the Zemindary to have been hereditary in the family of Bulwant Sing, a fact which I have never been able to aſcertain, though the Select Committee ſcruple not to aſſert, that it had deſcended to him from many generations. Cheyt Sing continued in the peaceable poſſeſſion of the Zemindary from 1770 to 1775, when the ſovereignty of Benares, without any conditions ſpecified in his favour, was transferred to the Company; and this again proves another error the Select Committee have fallen into, who ſay that it was transferred, ſubject as heretofore to the entire rule and management of Cheyt Sing. When I ſay Cheyt Sing was continued in the peaceable poſſeſſion of his Zemindary from 1770 to 1775, I beg to obſerve, that in that period he was called upon repeatedly for military aſſiſtance by the Vizier, and that he conſtantly furniſhed it independent of his annual rent, in conformity to the cuſtom of the Mogul empire, as will appear by the following extract of a letter from Cheyt Sing to the Governor General. " The great burthen of expence I laboured under from the time of the deceafe of the late Rajah, till the expiration of the Nabob Vizier's authority over me, is well known to God and your Excellency." In this letter Cheyt Sing undoubtedly alludes to the military aid he was bound to furnifh the Vizier. From 1775 to 1778, Cheyt Sing continued an obedient fubject to the Company. The Governor General and Council yielded to him the Cutwally and the Mint; but told him, that if he debafed the coin, he fhould be fubject to a fevere fine, and to *any other penalty they might think proper to impofe*. The Supreme Council aware of the importance of Benares, wrote as follows to the Court of Directors on the 7th of Auguft, 1775: "You will obferve, that the ceffion of the whole Zemindary of Cheyt Sing, with all the *powers and rights annexed to it*, is made immediately to the Eaft-India Company." Now, Sir, I would be glad to know what meaning you would affign to the terms *powers* and *rights*, and what they could mean, but the rights of fovereignty, of which the power of calling forth the military in time of need is furely the firft and the moft important — The letter I allude to was figned by all the Council, and General Clavering. Colonel Monfon and Mr. Francis in a feparate letter fay, that to them is due the credit of obtaining this important ceffion for the Eaft-India Company, entire and complete, and not held as Bengal is, by grant from the Mogul, as Duans.

I moft

I most earnestly entreat the attention of the Court to the following circumstances.

Our army continued on a peace establishment, from 1775 to July the 9th, 1778, and no military assistance was demanded from the Rajah. On that day intelligence being received of a war with France, it was determined by the Supreme Council to encrease our army very considerably, and to form a marine establishment for the defence of the Ganges—Upon considering from what funds these additional expences were to be defrayed, Mr Hastings proposed, "that Cheyt Sing be required in form, to contribute his share of the burthen of the present war, by consenting to the establishment of three regular battalions of Sepoys, to be raised and maintained at his expence." Mr. Francis acquiesced, but thought the demand should only be continued during the present war—Mr. Wheler agreed, wishing to avoid the question of right—Mr. Barwell agreed, supposing an acquisition of revenue and military force to have been annexed to the grant of the Zemindary. Mr. Hastings then adds, "He deems it a right inherent in every government. to impose such assessments as it judges expedient for the common service and protection of all its subjects." And adds, "*we are not precluded from it by any agreement subsisting between the Rajah and this government.*" The Rajah was written to, promised obedience; but having afterwards eluded his promise, the subject was again brought before the Board on the 28th of September, 1778: when

when Mr. Haſtings obſerved, "the evaſive conduct of the Rajah was owing to his having been adviſed to procraſtinate payment, on a ſuppoſition that a total change would take place in the government of Bengal, which would produce a repeal of the demand." On this occaſion the point of right was fully diſcuſſed; Mr. Francis expreſſed his doubts as to the juſtice of the demand, and he quoted a paragraph of Mr. Fowke's inſtructions, who was directed to inform the Rajah when he was inveſted with his Kellaut, "that ſo long as he adhered to his engagements, the Company would never demand any augmentation of the annual tribute which might be fixed." Mr. Haſtings's obſervation in reply was very remarkable; he ſays "the quotation from Mr. Fowkes' inſtructions related only to the *fixed and annual revenue*, but could never be underſtood *to preclude that right, which every government inherently poſſeſſes, to compel all its dependencies to contribute, by extraordinary ſupplies, to the relief of extraordinary emergencies.* The Board then determined to enforce the demand; and the money was paid. The minutes of theſe proceedings were tranſmitted to England; the ſubject was mentioned in the general letter, and the whole were received at the India Houſe in April and May 1779. It is ſomething extraordinary that a ſubject of ſuch importance, in which there had been a difference of opinion, ſhould never have drawn a line from the Directors. What is the concluſion — that they approved of the demand, but not being at that time, in the habit of expreſſing

their

their approbation of any act originating with Mr. Hastings, except that single one of *marching a detachment across India*, they were silent on the subject. Had the Directors thought the demand unjust; had they said, we differ from the Governor General's idea of the rights of sovereignty, and we think you have no claim upon Cheyt Sing, except for his annual tribute, the revolution of Benares could not have happened. The fact is, as you well know, that Acquiescence at that time was Approbation—But what follows is still more extraordinary: On the 19th of July, 1779, the war still continuing, Mr. Hastings proposed "that Cheyt Sing be again called upon to contribute his five lacks to the support of the increased establishment." The motion was unanimously agreed to, the Board being then complete by the arrival of Sir Eyre Coote. Cheyt Sing positively refused to pay the money; and Sir Eyre Coote, by order of the Board, directed two battalions of Sepoys to march to Benares to enforce the payment; when these troops arrived, the cash was paid, together with twenty thousand rupees, the extra expence of marching the detachment from Dinapore to Benares.

Intelligence of this extraordinory event was sent to England on the 14th of January, 1780. It arrived in October, and seems to have excited as little surprize here as it did in Bengal; for not the smallest notice was taken of the transaction by the Court of Directors; though the Governor General and Council, in their general letter, express their astonishment

at

at the refractory conduct of Cheyt Sing—I beg the Proprietors will attend to this circumstance.

On the 22d of June, 1780, the war still continuing, Mr. Hastings again proposed "that Cheyt Sing should be applied to for five lacks of rupees." It was unanimously agreed to. He promised instant compliance; and did pay one lack of rupees, but he delayed the payment of the remaining four lacks; and two lacks and a half of the money, the final balance, was not paid till the 18th of October, after a detachment had been ordered to Benares to enforce the payment. The account of this year's transactions was sent to England on the 29th of November, 1780, and received at the India House the 18th of October, 1781. I have never heard, Sir, that a single gentleman behind that bar has entered a protest against the proceedings of Mr. Hastings and his Council, to Cheyt Sing.—Will you then charge Mr. Hastings with being the sole cause of the revolution at Benares? If the demand (as most assuredly is the case) was just, it was right to enforce the payment of it—but if there are any gentlemen in the Direction who were *then* of a different opinion, how can they answer to the public in not bringing so important a point into full discussion, when a demand (according to the present doctrine) was made in direct violation of public faith, and enforced by military execution? Let me once more intreat the attention of the Court to this important subject, and to a circumstance, which, no doubt, will surprize them.

 I think

I think the Chairman has informed us, that of the five resolutions which Mr. Hastings has so solemnly denied to be founded in truth, the second passed the Court seventeen to two. In that resolution the Court of Directors say, that the Bengal government pledged itself that no other demand should be made upon Cheyt Sing beyond the payment of his stipulated tribute. Good God! Sir, are you aware of the conclusion to be drawn from this confession? To any or all of these seventeen gentlemen making such a confession, who were in the Direction in the years 1779, 1780, and 1781, do I attribute the revolution at Benares; and not to Mr. Hastings. He who solemnly asserting, Sir, on the 9th of July, and the 28th of September, 1778, that we were not prevented from making the extra demand upon Cheyt Sing by any engagement subsisting between us; who acting up to that solemn declaration, persisted in enforcing it for three years by military execution; who insisting upon it, that it was a right inherent in every state to impose such assessments on the subjects of that state as were necessary for the general defence; was neither to be bribed nor persuaded to relinquish what he deemed a just exaction—He, I say, Sir, acted from a firm conviction that he was right; and from 1778 to the present hour, his language has been uniform and consistent — Then what shall we say to you, Sir, and as many of the seventeen gentlemen as were Directors in 1779, 1780, and 1781, who conceiving that Mr. Hastings had so unwarrantably persisted in an unjust and oppressive demand; in a

demand

demand which brought on a rebellion, and ended in a revolution, yet never once protested against so glaring an act of injustice and oppression, or ever expressed the smallest disapprobation of his conduct? Shall we not say, Sir, that from the moment Mr. Hastings's conduct was made known to you and those gentlemen, who now assert that the government of Bengal has been guilty of an act of gross injustice, by extorting from Cheyt Sing what they could not have demanded without a violation of public faith; the responsibility of the measure rested with you? and that by not condemning his conduct, you caused the massacre of our troops—you caused the rebellion of Cheyt Sing—and you are the authors of the revolution of Benares. If the demand of extra aid, in time of war, had not been made for three successive years, the revolution of Benares would not have happened; nor would Mr. Hastings have persisted in it, had seventeen, or thirteen Directors commanded him to desist; and assured him, that according to their construction of our engagements, the demand was improper. If the business of Benares is not entered into, I shall say no more on the subject; but I am ready to meet your observations on Mr. Hastings's letter; and I shall now only add, that the Directors, if they act with justice, will repeal their second resolution; and then the only point to consider will be this—Was the fine of fifty lacks of rupees, which Mr. Hastings proposed to levy upon Cheyt Sing, too great for his offences. Mr. Hastings himself has brought forward his intention of fining Cheyt

 Sing,

Sing, who never did or could know of it; and I am ready at any time to meet this question.

You have been pleased, Mr. Chairman, to treat with an air of levity and ridicule Mr. Hastings's mode of negotiation — I have read the proceedings relative to the Maratta peace, from the instructions sent from Chunar to Colonel Muir, to Mr. Anderson's last letter; and I defy the greatest enemy Mr. Hastings has upon earth to read these valuable and important papers, without paying that tribute of praise to the Governor General, to which he is entitled, for the vigour, the firmness, the spirit, and the ability displayed through the whole course of the negotiation.

I do not mean to fatigue the Proprietors by reading extracts from the general letter; but having read it myself, I can assure them that it contains a full and complete explanation and justification of Mr. Hastings's conduct, as to those points which have been so severely animadverted upon in the Ninth Report of the Select Committee.*

Sir *Henry Fletcher* rose again, after Major Scott, and begged the indulgence of the Court while the

* See the paragraphs 50, 66, 67, 90, 91, 92, 93 94, 99, 100, 125, 126, 127, 128, 129, of the General Letter received by the Surprize packet, from Bengal.

Clerk

Clerk read certain paragraphs of a letter that he had brought forward for the consideration of the Court of Directors, and which, if approved by a majority, was to make part of the next general letter to Bengal. These paragraphs were accordingly read, and appeared to make a great impression upon the Proprietors, from the captious, unjust, and ungenerous reflections they contained on the conduct of the Governor General and Council, relative to the cession of Broach. When the Clerk had done reading—Mr. Sulivan rose in great emotion, and earnestly entreated the Proprietors to remember, that what had been read was the composition of the worthy Chairman, at least, that he had brought it forward—It neither had, nor could have, the sanction of the Court of Directors. That he had never read a letter of so pernicious a tendency; and he declared most solemnly, that if those paragraphs passed, there would be a third Maratta war—In the first place, the Chairman enters into a critique upon a transaction, of which, he confesses, all the materials are not before him. In the next place, he accuses the Supreme Council of cheating and deceiving the Peshwa; and lastly, he asks for that information, which he ought to have acquired before he attempted to animadvert upon the transaction; and when that information was received, he (Mr. Sulivan) was convinced, every difficulty would be as effectually cleared up in the mind of the Chairman as it then was in his own.

Governor *Johnstone* pressed the Chairman very much for an explanation, whether the three lacks relinquished by the 4th article of the treaty, and the lands ceded by Guickowar, mentioned in the 5th article, were not included in the account of the sixteen lacks collected by the establishment of Broach? To this the Chairman could give no distinct answer. But Mr. Hunter, one of the Directors, who had long been resident at Bombay, and who has generally possessed the most accurate advices, explained the matter to the Court, by stating, that six-tenths of the sixteen lacks had been ceded by the treaty; that there remained only seven lacks with the Company; that out of these seven lacks, one half had been promised to Sindia, and the other half to the Peshwa, at the convention of Worgaum; that it is true the Peshwa had relinquished the claim to his half by the late treaty; so that there remained three lacks and a half at the disposal of the India Company. Governor Johnstone then observed, that as the Chairman himself had acknowledged the civil establishment at Broach to cost three lacks, and the military three lacks more; supposing, upon the dominion being narrowed, our establishment to be brought to the lowest, still it must exceed five lacks; and therefore all we gave away, even by the Chairman's account, was one lack and a half — and this to secure the friendship of Madajee Sindia, the most powerful Chief in the Maratta empire; who, according to Mr. Hastings, had acted in the most steady, firm, and friendly manner throughout the whole negotiation. Besides, by this

relinquish-

relinquishment, we had removed the seeds of future discord; which were sown in a very plentiful soil indeed, if the English and the Marattas were to collect joint tribute in the same district, nay in the same villages. — The fate of Mr. Hastings is peculiarly hard — If he acquires dominion by conquest, upon aggression, he is stated to the world as acting from the lust of inordinate ambition and rapacity; if he yields the smallest territory in the spirit of peace and conciliation, and with a view of preserving those blessings, and rendering them permanent, he is held forth as dealing out kingdoms in profusion, without any regard to the emolument of the Company — but the one charge and the other are equally baffled, upon a close investigation. Governor Johnstone then proceeded to remark, with more warmth than he had shewn during the preceding part of the debate, that although he had been averse to calling the General Court, thinking the actions of Mr. Hastings in themselves greater than any eulogium that could be bestowed on them; and that the reproach of his enemies, and the reproach of public ministers, if they were his enemies, would fall much greater upon both, by taking no notice of the late advices; yet he now freely confessed his error — He saw why the opponents of Mr. Hastings were averse to the General Court; he saw also the propriety of its interference. When paragraphs, such as those which have been read, could be framed with such a captious, cavilling spirit; conceived in language so unworthy the Court of Directors, and so unfit to be sent to the Governor

General

General of Bengal at any time when he held ſuch a commiſſion; and much more after tranſmitting accounts of events that muſt command the gratitude and admiration of future ages, if it could not extinguiſh the malicious ſpirit of thoſe who endeavoured to vilify his character by the groſſeſt miſrepreſentations, in ſcenes with which the public at large are not intimately acquainted, where the tranſactions were ſo complicated that few could unravel them. That it became more neceſſary now to enforce the motion, and even to invite oppoſition, which he before deprecated, that the merits of the queſtion might be tried by the moſt ſolemn deciſion.

Sir Henry Fletcher defended the letter, thought the ſtyle was decent and proper, and that the Directors had a right to demand an explanation in the terms he had uſed.

Mr. *Watſon.*

Sir Henry Fletcher,

I SHOULD not have intruded upon the patience of the Court, in this ſtage of the debate, if I did not think it exceedingly for the intereſt of the East-India Company, and equally for the honour of the Britiſh name, that the propoſed vote of approbation and thanks ſhould paſs unanimouſly. All the weight of argument, upon the ſubſtantial merits of the queſtion, ſeems to me to have been on one ſide only,

 and

and therefore I will not repeat what was urged so ably by the honourable Governor who opened the debate, and by my learned friend who seconded the motion, least, in the repetition, I should exhaust the spirit of their remarks. What has occupied the attention of gentlemen for the last half hour, is a very light feather indeed in the opposite scale. Let us advert for a moment, to what the real topic of discussion is; I take it to be this: Whether Mr. Hastings, supported by the other members of the Supreme Council, was the cause of those effectual supplies to the Carnatic, which enabled the forces and friends of the East-India Company to hold out, till the face of affairs was altered by the Maratta peace; whether he was the author and framer of that peace; and whether that peace be such, under all its circumstances, as to deserve censure or praise.

By the turn which the debate has taken, the whole subject matter of this enquiry is narrowed to the last question only. I have not heard it disputed, that for the large supplies sent to Madras, to the amount, if I mistake not, of about three millions sterling, we are indebted to the spirited exertions of the Governor General and Council of Bengal. No man has this day raised a suspicion, that uncommon ability and exertion have not been uniformly displayed by the Governor General Council, during the late hostilities in India; no man has denied the effectual support received from them, under the most pressing difficulties, towards carrying on the war in the

Carnatic. Indeed it ſeems undeniable, that their conduct upon the moſt trying occaſions, that of the Governor General in particular, has diſplayed ſuch wiſdom, penetration, and magnanimity, as do not uſually fall to the lot of mortals. It has not been contradicted that the ſucceſſes of Hyder's irruption were checked by that great man; or, that in all probability, the completion of thoſe exertions will anihilate the dangerous power of the French, and of thoſe natives whoſe enmity to us has been encouraged by their alliance all over India. I have not heard a doubt ſtarted from any quarter, but that the concluſion of this treaty of peace with the Marattas, at ſo critical a period, has nearly compleated the triumph of our arms in India, or has at leaſt totally prevented the triumph of thoſe of our enemies. I have not heard it doubted, much leſs have I heard it denied, that the plan of peace was laid by Mr. Haſtings, that the definitive concluſion of it was obtained by his perſeverance, and the able negotiation of Mr. Anderſon, who was choſen out by him for this great work. I have, indeed, with ſome amazement, heard it imputed to Mr. Haſtings, that this was not the only plan which ſuggeſted itſelf to his active mind. I have, with increaſe of aſtoniſhment, heard it contended, that therefore ſucceſs was not to have been expected from his ſuperabundant endeavours, and accordingly that our thanks for his having accompliſhed that ſucceſs, may, with reaſon, be delayed. Thus, Sir, we are deſired to make the activity of his exertions, not barely an

apology,

apology, but a reaſon for the ſlowneſs of our praiſe. Yet, admitting the utmoſt that is, or can be contended; admitting that it was not a wiſe plan laid by Mr. Haſtings for General Goddard to lead his army from Bengal, through the very heart of the Maratta dominions, and ſo attended, to treat for peace at Poona, the capital. Granting that this negotiation would not have been ſucceſsful, even if the convention of Worgaum had not operated, like a chilling froſt to nip it in the bud; granting likewiſe that the Rajah of Berar was an improper perſon to have been treated with; that it would have been impolitic and unjuſt to place him at the head of the Maratta government; and that Mr. Haſtings was at one moment weak enough to think of propoſing this wrong to be done to the preſent Peſhwa, as the condition of obtaining terms of peace in other reſpects honourable. All theſe things being allowed, what has been, or what can be made of them as reaſons for poſtponing our vote of commendation for the peace actually obtained, and the other honourable ſervices ſpecified in the motion, why, nothing more than this: that two treaties being opened, beſides that which has been finally concluded, once afforded reaſon for ſuſpecting that no peace would ſoon be ratified. But is it, Sir, perfectly fair to argue from hence, that gratitude ſhould ſleep, now ſo glorious a peace is in fact concluded, in point of time ſo early, and on terms ſo advantageous, beyond our moſt ſanguine expectations? Is it right to ſift the active workings of this great man's mind, to

 ſcrutinize

ſcrutinize the trials made by him in different quarters, and diſcovering (what he had before diſcovered) that the obſtacles to ſome of them were ſo many, as to render ſucceſs doubtful, therefore, to deny him commendation for ceaſing to purſue unſucceſsful endeavours too far, and for graſping at the aſtoniſhing idea of compelling Madajee Sindia to be the mediator and guarantee of permanent tranquillity, by ſending the vigour of war into the heart of this powerful chief's dominions, by attacking his capital, by calling his whole attention to his own immediate danger, and thereby convincing him, that unleſs by ſuing for peace, he could not ſave himſelf from ruin, and his name from being obliterated from the roll of Maratta chiefs, except when Mr. Haſtings ſhould be mentioned as the cauſe of its being expunged? Ought the Governor General to be blamed for this, eſpecially when, upon Sindia's deſiring terms of peace for himſelf, by the wiſeſt exerciſe of good policy, peace was granted to him upon condition of his becoming the mediator with the Poona Durbar, and with the other powerful chiefs of the Maratta State, for accompliſhing a general pacification? Let us firſt ſee if it be poſſible to fix a ſtandard in our own minds, by which to meaſure ſuch great conceptions before we begin to arraign them in the groſs, or to develope their parts, in order to find little faults with ſome of them. And reſpecting which faults, if they be ſuch, when all is ſaid, the truth turns out, that they are, at the utmoſt, ſuch ſlight deviations from perfection

 itſelf,

itself, as only serve to mark that Mr. Hastings is still a man; for to err is the fault of human nature. But the errors of Mr. Hastings, in this business of the Maratta peace, appear to me excessively trivial, when compared with those wonderful exertions of human intellect, and that steadiness to his point, by which it was at length perfected, and the ratification finally exchanged, upon terms that must perpetuate his abilities and name in all parts of the world whither the annals which inrol the transaction may reach, down to the latest hour of their preservation. I did hardly expect to hear the European treaty of peace, the sickness or the death of Hyder, or the intervention of any other circumstances that might possibly concur in forwarding this glorious peace, made use of in argument to diminish from the merit of Mr. Hastings in getting it accomplished. As the matter strikes my mind, one peculiar merit which distinguishes Mr. Hastings as a compleat statesman in this business is, his catching at all favourable circumstances as they arose, and improving them to the great purpose he had in view. And before I can be qualified to find fault, I must have my mind raised to the elevation of his. I know, indeed, that little minds can censure, what, from human imperfection, the greatest cannot mend. I refer now to the manner of his attaining the object at which we have so much cause to rejoice; and do not refer to any distinct acts of Mr. Hastings's administration. I am not his general advocate; I think he has his errors, and great ones. When I saw the dreadful mischiefs

of

of ſuch a war as was carrying on with the Maratta country, conſidering him as the author of that war, no man was more free to cenſure him; and I muſt ſee the evidence of his being, or not being ſo, in a very different light from that in which it ever has appeared to me, and yet does appear to me, before I can retract that cenſure. But let not this prevail with me to refuſe him my warmeſt gratitude and applauſe for the Maratta peace. No man has denied to me that this peace is peculiarly his — excluſively his in the planning — and carried on to its completion under his firm inſtructions, by his choſen inſtruments. I blamed, and ſtill do blame him, for the war; but I think him entitled, in a tenfold degree, to my warmeſt thanks for this peace. I will examine a little more particularly whether he is ſo: and the rule I will go by ſhall be the only objection which I underſtand to be now relied on. Indeed we were told that a ſecret article was ſigned, between Sindia and the Peſhwa, on the very day that the definitive treaty of peace was interchanged. But we are not told that it is an article injurious to us; and it may be ſome matter relative to their mutual intereſts, as contradiſtinguiſhed from the other Maratta powers. This, however, and an account of the capture of two officers by the Marattas, in their way to General Matthews, ſince the ſigning of the articles, (which muſt have ariſen from ſome miſtake; but which, if it ſhould turn out as at preſent related, can hardly be conſidered as an infraction of the treaty) were ſlightly mentioned, as reaſons for poſtponing

the

the vote now under consideration. But they seem to be given up. And the only objection persisted in is, that by way of bargain with Sindia, the half of Broach was promised, upon condition of his securing the peace; and that on the day of its final settlement the whole was, by a secret article, actually given up to him, and not merely the half stipulated for. This introduced some discussions about the real value of Broach; estimates have been read; actual receipts have been stated — Whether half was not ceded to the Marattas by the treaty itself, and whether the Mogul half was not all we had to give afterwards, and consequently all that was given Sindia by the secret articles, and whether even this was not his before, according to the stipulation made with him for saving our Bombay army, have been started as questions, upon which the affirmative has been presumed, remains uncontradicted. As I understand the fact, the Mogul share of the city of Broach is by the treaty retained to the Company, exempted from every claim of chout. — The Maratta country of three lacks near Broach as ceded to us by Colonel Upton's treaty, is relinquished to them again — and the Guickwar lands are restored to the two Guickwars and to the Peshwa, to be apportioned according to the real truth of their respective original claims. And I likewise conceive that the Mogul share is the douceur given to Scindia for his agency in the peace. But I will not consider the matter upon these grounds. I love to meet an objection fairly, and to examine it upon its broadest preten-

sions.

ſions. Whether therefore ſixteen or ſix lacks be the real value of the city and territory of Broach — whether the whole or the half of this, the Mogul or the Maratta ſhare, be which it may, or both be the price paid for the Maratta peace, ſhall make no part of my argument. But is this peace, under all the other circumſtances of obtaining it, upon the whole, too dearly purchaſed at any price alledged to be given for it? This is now the only queſtion. I have heard it often ſaid, that any peace in India is better than any war. The point has been diſcuſſed upon records, with uncommon ability, between Mr. Haſtings and a gentleman of whoſe integrity I entertain the higheſt opinion, whoſe minutes do equal honour to his head and heart, and for whom I have the higheſt perſonal reſpect. I have alſo very frequently heard the ſame thing aſſerted in this country. And although it is not perhaps a propoſition univerſally true, in the moſt abſolute ſenſe, yet I have never entertained a doubt, that any peace likely to be laſting, procured upon any terms, would be better than the late actual war which threatened our total extirpation from India, or at any rate endangered our ſettlements both on the Coromandel and Malabar coaſts. What, Sir, have the Governor General and Council obtained to relieve us from ſuch apprehenſions? A peace, highly honourable and beneficial; at the price, if you pleaſe, of giving up all the Broach revenues, whatever the amount of them may be. A peace in which although Baſſein is delivered up to the Peſhwa, Salſette, and other places, of greater importance to the Company

pany than Baſſein, are retained in our poſſeſſion — A peace wherein the reſpective allies of the two parties to the treaty are included with them; except that Hyder Ally, before in alliance with the Peſhwa, ſhould, now at the riſkof forfeiting that alliance, be made to relinquiſh and reſtore to the Company, and their allies, all poſſeſſions taken by him from either. In ſhort Hyder was by the terms of this peace to be compelled to abſtain from his hoſtilities — And all the Chiefs of the Maratta State are included in the treaty, and bound by it — former privileges of trade are reſtored on all ſides — the enemies of one are to be holden enemies of the other — Madajee Sindia, who was the mediator, became the guarantee of this treaty, thus accompliſhed; and the queſtion now is, whether at the price paid to him, alledged to be a city and territory of ſixteen lacks, the purchaſe is too dear — My anſwer is, that the annual expences of your army to carry on the war, prodigiouſly exceeded the largeſt eſtimate that has been named as the conſideration given for the peace; and your all was at ſtake; every poſſeſſion you have was in hourly riſk and danger. But before the ink of the treaty was well dry, one of the articles had wrought its effect. It will be recollected that Tippo Saib ſucceeded to the command of the Myſore army, upon the death of his father, Hyder Ally, in December laſt, the very month in which this treaty (that had been concluded between Madajee Sindia and Mr. Anderſon in May, and ratified by the Governor General and Council in June) was completely ratified by the miniſters at

Poona; Tippo was pursuing the footsteps of his father, but was so suddenly checked in his career, by the article which expressly named Hyder, that in March, within three weeks after the Definitive Treaty was finally interchanged with public formalities, he was actually retreating with his army home to Mysore, with all possible expedition. We understand it to be indubitably certain, that on the 13th of March our troops took possession of Arcot, for the Nabob, within an hour after it was evacuated by Tippo Saib. We know by the same authority, that he no longer holds Arneè — in a word that he has left the Carnatic — and that the full and final settlement of peace with the Marattas, and most peculiarly and emphatically this article in the alliance with them respecting Hyder, had an instantaneous effect upon Tippo Saib, his son and successor, equivalent to a total overthrow. The Maratta Ministers and Chiefs agreed to compel him to make peace; and upon his refusal, to join in the requisite measures for his utter ruin. He instantly felt the effect of this alliance between them, and as suddenly retired. As to this one article, therefore, we have decisive knowledge of the instantaneous good effect of the treaty. Can we then with the smallest propriety suspend our vote of thanks, with the avowed purpose of waiting to know the effect of the treaty, and no other? This would be a tacit disapprobation of the whole of this article, as well as the rest; it would weaken the confidence of our friends, raise the spirits of our enemies, and among other mischie-

vous

vous consequences, provoke the former to with-hold their assistance, and the latter to renew their attacks. Such a waiting as this for beneficial effects from the peace, and a suspension of our thanks till they all take place, may make a change in this instance of Tippo — may prevent the other good effects entirely, and must necessarily retard their progress, which it is alike for our interest and our honour to accelerate. But notwithstanding we have been barely desired to suspend our vote of praise, the only argument that is relied upon, implies that a vote of censure ought to be passed; and this is the more manly way of putting the case: — the purchase of this peace is more than it is worth; or, in the mildest form of considering the subject, better terms might have been obtained; and therefore the large revenues of Broach ought not to have been given up, as the price of it, to the mediator and guarantee. In discussing this matter, one thing ought to be considered: that in all negotiations of this nature there must be some inducement to a compliance on each side, or they never can terminate in an agreement. In this instance I have said before, that, admitting, for the sake of argument, the city and territory of Broach to produce sixteen lacks, though I take the fact to be most decisively otherwise) and admitting the whole of this to have been reserved to the Company by the treaty, (though upon the face of the treaty itself I take this not to have been so either) and that by a secret article with Sindia, voluntarily offered, after the ratification, beyond the bounty stipulated for, the whole of this revenue is confirmed to him, by as permanent a tenure as the definitive treaty of which he is the guarantee; all this amounts to but a small proportion of the sum annually expended in the war. And therefore allowing this to be really the price, I should not think it wantonly squandered away, but the termination of the war would, in my opinion, be purchased at a cheap rate: for it is no less than salvation from utter destruction. It bids fair to be as permanent as it is extensive; or if it should not be so, the blame will be most probably due to ourselves. But then we have been asked, What will the Peshwa, the Ministers, and other Chiefs say, when they find that by the secret article with Sindia, their share of the revenues of Broach is given over to him? I can only answer, that if by the definitive treaty of peace the Guickwar country is given back to its former owners, and whatever was formerly a part of the Peshwa's territories is restored to him, this secret article cannot operate upon either, but extends only to the Mogul share, which the Company were to possess, and therefore might dispose of, without participation or claim of any kind; on the other hand, if by the definitive treaty the whole is reserved to the English, then whether they use it themselves, or give it up to another as a reward for equivalent services, no just offence can be taken by the other parties to the treaty.

Upon the whole, Sir, if Mr. Hastings and the Council General deserve our thanks at all, I can see no objection against agreeing to the entire resolution

proposed.

proposed. The latter part, in particular, appears to me the necessary result of the former; since it would be the height of folly to commend the Governor General for what he has done, and at the same time to wish for his recal before he has compleated the work. To request his continuance in the government, and at the same time to with-hold from him our most vigorous support, would be still a more extreme degree of folly, and would savour so much of dislike to the admirable peace he has obtained, as to take away all confidence which Sindia may have in us, or our nation, to betray total want of public faith, and to endanger the renewal of the Maratta war, accompanied by fresh irruptions from every power of India that heretofore has been inimical to the English, or may be desirous to drive us from our settlements.

This is my sincere opinion. I do not know how to argue upon it more at large, after it has been discussed with so much greater ability. I cannot feel the force of what has been urged against it, and I think that I have considered the objection dispassionately. I will not fatigue the Court by repeating those arguments which have been urged in its favour, with infinitely greater abilities than I possess. My only motive for rising was to enforce the remark with which I began, and in the propriety of which I am confirmed by every thing that I have heard, that it is equally for our interest and our honour to pass this resolution unanimously. It may be collected,

collected, from what I have already offered, that I am not misled into this sentiment by any undue predilection in favour of Mr. Hastings. I am actuated merely as a public man, and purely upon public motives. I am very far from commending all the actions of his life, or approving all the measures of his government; but I will not, in this hour of rejoicing, undertake the invidious task of bringing forward any matter extraneous to the immediate question before us, which might be an alloy to the praises justly due to the astonishing success of his wonderful exertions. To deny him these praises would be to dishonour myself. I am not his general panegyrist; I have no personal attachment to him; and if I feel any prejudice, it is against him; but were I capable of the most mortal enmity, and he the object of it, I hope that I should not even then be so deficient in the first rudiments of public virtue, as to refuse my vote of commendation and applause, to him and his colleagues, for such distinguished services, so gloriously performed.—If I were, my case would, according to my poor apprehension, resemble that of some captious mortal, refusing to thank Heaven for the vivifying power of the sun, after the storms of winter, because spots have been discovered on its surface.

The question was now called for from all parts of the court; but Mr. Edward Moore being upon his legs, Governor Johnstone earnestly desired to be heard, to order: He said he entreated the Proprietors

to

to liſten with the utmoſt attention to what the honourable and worthy gentleman, Mr. Moore, ſhould ſay. Let them conſider the advantages their enemies would take of them, were they now to call for the queſtion. The preſent meeting which in point of numbers, and of the honourable characters who filled the court, was as reſpectable an aſſembly as had ever been convened in that or any other place, would be termed a factious, diſorderly aſſembly. He therefore begged the Proprietors to attend to whatever might fall from the honourable gentleman, or any other Proprietor who was an enemy to the motion.

General *Oglethorpe.*

I BEG, Sir Henry Fletcher, to be heard, to order: The debate has taken ſo extraordinary a turn, that I entreat every gentleman preſent will liſten with attention to the worthy Proprietor. The point now is, whether you approve or diſapprove of the Maratta peace; and I am exceedingly anxious to obtain every information I can on that important ſubject—as a worthy Director has ſaid, " if we approve of the Chairman's proceedings, we ſhall have a third Maratta war."

Mr.

Governor *Johnstone* having introduced his motion of of thanks to Mr. Haſtings, without reading any papers or extracts from the Company's records, or adduced any premiſes whereon to found concluſions to warrant his motion, Mr. E. Moore roſe and expreſſed his ſurpriſe at the Governor's mode of proceeding, and wiſhed to have ſuch documents produced, as might enable him and the Court to form a judgment on the very extenſive and *complicated* queſtion before them. This cauſed Governor Johnſtone to ſay, he meant, before he ſat down, to call for certain extracts and papers to be read ſhort, for the information of the court. Mr. Moore complained of the Governor's retrograde method of proceeding, in firſt introducing his motion, telling the Proprietors it could not poſſibly meet with a diſſentient voice; and then calling for a few *detatched paragraphs* in the Company's diſpatches, to be read ſhort, when, in order to judge of the propriety of the queſtion before them, it was neceſſary to ranſack the Company's records ten years back. Mr. Moore ſaid, calling for *detatched parts*, and not the *whole of the proceedings* againſt Cheyt Sing, was one part of Mr. Haſtings's complaint againſt the Court of Directors, in his letter of the 20th March, 1783; becauſe, without *the whole* proceedings had been before the Directors, Mr. Haſtings tells them it was impoſſible they could judge of his conduct in that buſineſs.

 From

From Mr. Haſtings's own doctrine, it ſhews how neceſſary it is to have the *whole* hiſtory of Mr. Haſtings's conduct in the Maratta war before the Court, before they can poſſibly be ripe to judge of a motion of thanks to him for concluding the Maratta peace. He obſerved, that in the extracts and papers the Governor meant to call for, he took no notice of Mr. Haſtings's letter to the Court of Directors of the 20th of March, and inſiſted, that was too material a paper to eſcape the attention of the Court of Proprietors; for it contained a direct and abſolute *charge* againſt the Court of Directors, a charge, which their honour and the duty they owed to the Company, called upon them to anſwer; for it was little ſhort of a criminal accuſation. Therefore, he preſſed the Chairman to know, whether he, the whole Court of Directors, or any one of them, had prepared any anſwer to that letter, or could ſay any thing in juſtification of their conduct, ſo directly criminated by the Governor General's letter. This, but not till repeatedly preſſed, drew from the Chairman, Sir Henry Fletcher, an account of what he had prepared as an anſwer, and conceived to be a compleat juſtification of the Directors, in oppoſition to the Governor General's charge. This very material information, threw ſuch light upon the queſtion, that Mr. Moore inſiſted, nothing but the moſt determined reſolution of the Court, blindly to vote for the motion of thanks, without information, could induce the honourable mover (after hearing this juſtification of the Chairman read) to hope for uccefs in carrying it. The enormous bribe of two hundred thoufand pounds per annum, given to Sindia, the guarantee of the treaty, for his fervices in bringing it to a conclufion, was enough to damn the peace and the peace-maker: This two hundred thoufand pounds per annum, the only advantageous article of the treaty, ought to have come into the Company's coffers, not into Scindia's. This, and this only, was fufficient, without the unknown fecret article, or any other circumftance, to evince the neceffity of poftponing the vote of thanks, till the Court was ripe, from a confideration of the whole of Mr. Haftings's conduct, and various circumftances attending the negociations for the Maratta peace, to judge of the queftion before them. He charged Governor Johnftone, who had mentioned Lord Rodney's cafe, with judging from *events,* and not *circumftances,* infifting that Lord Rodney's difmiffion from the public fervice, at the moment it was determined, might be wife and perfectly well judged; and that his Lordfhip's fortunate conqueft afterwards, was *an event,* which ought not to weigh a feather, in oppofition to fuch a determination. That in like manner the various cenfures, voted by parliament, the Directors, and Proprietors, upon Mr. Haftings, were warranted, juft, and proper, at the moment; and that the *event* of the Maratta peace, however fortunate it had been, (though he contended it was a difgrace both to the Company and the nation) could not *now* wipe away, nor bury in oblivion, the crimes for which he had been formerly cenfured;

and he insisted, the premises from which the Governor attempted to draw his conclusions, was an absurd mode of reasoning, condemned by every day's experience. It was true we had a peace with the Marattas, but it was replete with disgrace, and instead of obtaining the object which induced the managers of it to break the peace settled by Colonel Upton, they had been obliged to relinquish the advantages of that treaty. Never were the British arms and name so degraded, so tarnished, as by the breach of Upton's treaty and the terms of the present; to say nothing of a loss of four millions of money, in the prosecution of it, which had drained their eastern treasuries of every rupee.

He said, the honourable Governor had laid great stress on the ninth article of the treaty respecting Hyder Ally; and the thirteenth article respecting their intercourse with the European nations, as advantages compensating every relinquishment on the part of the Company. This language, he said, was very well calculated to impose on the uninformed Proprietors; but gentlemen who had been in India knew it to be a fact, that the Marattas and Hyder were natural enemies.—(the Governor and others affected to laugh at this) He added, it is only a want of acquaintance with the history and interest of the various Asiatic powers, that occasions this laugh: every gentleman around me, who has been in the east, cannot be ignorant, there is an infinitely greater natural antipathy between the Marattas and Hyder, than between the English and French; and it was the enormities of Mr. Hastings, that drove th m into an alliance against us, for their mutual defence and safety. They were at war against each other, and joined their arms to seek revenge against us. Nay, to such an height were their hostilities carried, that Hyder even went so far as to call on us to join him against the Marattas, in virtue of our treaty of 1769. The madness of government refused; and, in so doing, broke that treaty, *by not going to war with the Marattas*; and in Bengal, your government, or rather governor, broke a second treaty, Colonel Upton's, made under the direction of those able and virtuous men, Sir J. Clavering, Monson, and Francis, *by going to war with them*. From these inconsistencies and infirmities in your Councils, and from their disregard to national honour and faith, these two Indian powers, Hyder and the Marattas, which no cement could ever unite before, were driven to a junction for their mutual protection, as well as to punish our perfidy; no other conjuncture, no other combination of causes could possibly have effected so unnatural an union. Hence there can be no great merit, as the honourable mover of this question would have us believe, due to Mr. Hastings for this article: so contrary to it, that people in Bengal are astonished the Marattas did not condition with your Governor General for Hyder's extirpation; and such appears to be the latent intent of the ninth article of the Maratta treaty.

With

With regard to the thirteenth article, respecting intercourse between the Marattas and European powers: This article, also, is not less their own inclination and interest than ours; and most likely was a proposition of their own, me ing thereby to plead the sanctity of treaty for obviating the importunity of European powers without giving offence. The Marattas abhor the idea of intermixing with European nations, as much as christians do living amongst infidels. Their religious tenets, manners, and customs, forbid; and their national interests will ever oppose it. The Chevalier St. Lubin, who was intriguing at the court of Poonah, on the part of the French, for four or five years, never once received the faintest shade of encouragement; although his being there was matter of great suspicion to your government in Bengal, and one reason amongst other very inadmissible ones, for the origin of the late Maratta war.

Great errors in oriental management, arise from a want of uniformity in system. By the causes of the present war with Hyder and the Marattas, it appears we have had as many systems as governments; and that each government has had a system of its own; in so much, that while the government of Madrass broke a treaty *by not going to war with the Marattas*; the government of Bengal broke a treaty *by going to war with them.* It will be worth observing, how this treaty with the Marattas is worded, and particularly the preamble or title. It never once mentions the name of Mr. Hastings, and *emphatically* confines the appointment of the *Governor General and Council, to the King and Parliament of Great Britain*, making them the representatives of the nation at large, and the tutelary guardian of the East India Company's right only, without other responsibility towards them. This is virtually denying them any controuling jurisdiction; the whole treaty breaths nothing but contrition and submission, and more properly to be stiled *entreaty*. The reason of this extraordinary departure from the real constitution of the Company's government is, that *Sindia*, the guarantee, and surety for our future good behaviour, was so enraged at Mr. Hastings's perfidy and intrigue, that he would not bear to hear his name mentioned: this fact is well known in India. No doubt this peace with the Marattas, disgraceful as it is, in point of submissive relinquishment of right and acquisition, has its advantages; of securing Bengal from their inroads, and a general combination of all oriental powers, and retrenchment of great expences, the continuance of which, threatened to drain the Asiatic settlements of the last particle of specie. But these are not the meritorious gifts of the peace-maker,—yet, to my surprise and astonishment, though the gentleman who supports this motion, admits Mr. Hastings to be the author of the Maratta war; great merit and applause is attributed to him, as the basis whereon they build this motion of thanks and public favour. If such, then, are the advantages, the merits, the desirable blessings of peace, why go unprovoked to war? Why plunge

and

and drown all those inestimable blessings in wild, headstrong schemes of visionary conquest? Why violate the rights of nations, sacrifice every pinciple of humanity, and trample on the natural rights of mankind? And why infract the peace of Poorunder, settled by Colonel Upton in 1776, the terms of which were *honourable and advantageous to the Company*, and met the highest and most distinguished approbation of the nation? Was it because that treaty was effected by the well-timed interposition of the virtuous administration of Sir John Clavering, Monson, and Francis? I think the last as probable a reason as any. If Mr. Hastings's advocates would ingenuously acknowledge his errors, in commencing this war, he would then be entitled to every commendation due to the merit of his reform; but in no other point of view can they assume to claim it. Indeed the honourable Governor acknowledges Mr. Hastings was not free from errors; but says, Mr. Hastings's merits in making this peace, ought to be a veil and cover for them, and desires they may be forgot. I have minutes in my hand, by which I see I have met him in this court ten years ago. I shall be happy to meet him here ten years hence: these minutes remind me of what the honourable Governor wishes me and this court to forget; namely, that on the 6th December, 1775, Mr. Hastings was censured by this court, for being the author of an unjust and unprovoked war against the Rohillas, — a people ever considered as a barrier between us and the Marattas.

That on the 2d April 1776, Mr. Hastings was

censured for suffering his banyan to hold farms, contrary to the regulations of the Committee of Revenue in Bengal, — for suffering Cantoo Baboo to withdraw his security, &c. by which the Company incurred a loss of 500,000l.

That on the 8th May, 1776, Mr. Hastings and Mr. Barwell's conduct was such, it was resolved by the directors, to remove them from their respective offices.

That when this question was agitated in the General Court of Proprietors, the misfortune was, that Mr. Hastings and Mr. Barwell being both included in *one* question, it proved the salvation of Mr. Barwell, who, upon his own confession, was universally condemned; and, had the question been put separately, Mr. Barwell would certainly have been removed, and his removal would again have put the Government into the hands of Sir John Clavering and Mr. Francis, under whose conduct the Company's affairs flourished, and arrived at that height of prosperity and glory, from which, since Colonel Monson's demise, they have ever been falling, under Mr. Hastings's government.

My minute, likewise reminds me, that on Nov. 19, 1776, we were assembled to consider of a letter from Mr. Hastings, wherein he had authorised, impowered and directed Mr. Maclean to signify his resignation. This resignation was unanimously approved by the Court of Directors; and Mr. Maclean said he would suffer crucifixion if Mr. Hastings did not resign. Can this Court forget Mr. Hastings's conduct on that occasion? On that very day, I ventured

tured to aſſert, ſpeaking of Sir J. Clavering, Monſon, and Francis, that they had been the ſaviours of the country, and of the property of the Company and individuals — That they had improved the country; increaſed your collections; augmented your inveſtments; reduced your expences; effected treaties (amongſt which the Maratta was one) which ſupported one-third of your military eſtabliſhment; and ſtill more, paid off all your bond debts, which threated your ruin. — Nor can I forget, that the honourable Governor, who generally contrives to laugh at what falls from me, was happy in his laugh on that occaſion — But, he muſt now ſuffer me to bring to his ſerious attention, what happened in 1780, when he was very active in the appointment of Lord Macartney to the government of Madras: an appointment that did him and every man who joined their efforts to his, in obtaining it, great honour; for Lord Macartney's abilities, integrity, good management, and virtue, has endeared him to this Company, and his country, in a way never to be forgotten. Does the honourable Governor and this Court recollect, that in ſupport of Lord Macartney's nomination to Madras, the Governor ſaid, " Never, will I again oppoſe the nomination of a Governor to any of our ſettlements who has not been brought up in your ſervice, for that reaſon only; for when I conſider the abilities, the virtues, the unſkaken integrity, and great ſervices of Sir John Clavering, whoſe ſtatue ought now to be before us in Gold, I muſt ever lament the oppoſition I gave to his meaſures." —— The honourable Governor, in opening his motion this day, has told you, "The thanks he wishes to vote for Mr. Hastings may be considered as an implied censure upon others; and has endeavoured to explain that away." I have formerly said it, in this Court, and shall ever insist, that the honourable Governor's eulogium upon General Clavering was, by fair implication, a *severe censure upon Mr. Hastings's* conduct, who in his letter to the Court of Directors, December 3, 1774, protests against all the acts of the majority of the Council, then composed of Clavering, Monson, and Francis. Let us compare our *present* situation with our former upon the death of Colonel Monson, when your present Governor General became all powerful.

The honourable mover of the question before us, gives great merit to Mr. Hastings for the pecuniary supplies he sent to Madrass. How were those supplies raised? By stopping all issues from your Bengal treasury; accumulating all your collections in January, February, and March 1783; by every exertion, and draining every resource, Mr. Hastings was able to send ten lacks of Rupees with Sir Eyre Coote to Madras. Ten lacks was all that could be got in these three months; though it is a fact known in Bengal, that by a judicious management of your revenues there, the month of January only ought to have produced sixty lacks. — In March 1783, our situation in Bengal was nearly as follows — Not a Rupee in the treasury — The country in ruins — The revenues collected in March had fallen short near sixty lacks; and no prospect of any more for three or four months to come — Your investments

only

only provided for payment of a million of money and upwards, borrowed in Bengal, and drawn upon the Company, payable here—Your expences in Bengal daily increasing — Treaties made that disgrace you — Your military and civil establishments many months in arrear; the money that ought to have paid them, and purchased your investments, having been squandered away in the unprovoked, unjust, unnecessary Maratta war — Your armies ready to mutiny, for want of pay in March — The Company at home not in a capacity to accept the bills drawn for the investments; and besides, owing above one million to Government for customs they are not able to pay.

I intreat you to contrast this picture with the state of your affairs when they fell under Mr. Hastings's direction in 1776, and then say, whether Mr. Hastings deserves your thanks.—Though you may doubt these facts to-day, before this day twelve months you will, I fear, be convinced they are too true. If they are true, where can you look for, and how can you hope for that dividend which will be due in January next?—I wish to protect my property; and, if my fellow proprietors have any regard for theirs, they cannot any longer support the man who has brought this company to the brink of ruin. I observe the honourable Director on the right hand of the chair (Mr. Sulivan) says, the Chairman's answer to the Governor General's letter is no justification of the directors, and that it would be a dangerous letter to send to India.—And he reminds us of Mr. Hastings's services to the Company, in increaſing the ſalt farms ſixty lacks,—but forgets Mr. Haſtings ſuffered his banyan to hold ſome of theſe farms for his benefit. — I have not much confidence in what falls from that gentleman; for I well remember, that on the eve of our bankruptcy ten years ago, he ſtood up, in the very place where he now is, and aſſured us, all would do well, and nothing was wanting but a *little circulation*; though, in a ſhort time after, the Company were inſolvent.—A learned gentleman (Mr. Dallas) has juſt acknowledged, that Mr. Haſtings's friendſhip induced him to give the honourable Director's ſon a valuable contract, for which he had been blamed.—No wonder, then, that the honourable Director is Mr. Haſtings's panegyriſt! The ſin of ingratitude is a damnable ſin! But, it cannot be imputed to the honourable Director.—I requeſt the Court will remember, though they do not regard what has fallen from me this day; for, ſure I am, it will be neceſſary to remind them of it hereafter, when it will be too late for them to correct the error they are ſo very impatient to commit. I will only add, that I lay my hand upon my heart, and aſſure the Court, the negative I ſhall give to this queſtion, proceeds from the perfect conviction in my own mind, that there are not the leaſt grounds, upon which Mr. Haſtings is entitled to our thanks.

When Mr. Moore ſat down, the queſtion was again called; and, no other gentleman riſing to ſpeak, it was put by the Chairman, and carried with only a ſingle negative,—Mr. Edward Moore's.

THE END.

www.ingramcontent.com/pod-product-compliance
Lightning Source LLC
Chambersburg PA
CBHW030537270326
41927CB00008B/1418
* 9 7 8 3 3 3 7 0 1 2 5 6 4 *